Comfort
& Spice

Comfort & Spice

NIAMH SHIELDS

LYONS PRESS
Guilford, Connecticut
An imprint of Globe Pequot Press

To buy books in quantity for corporate use
or incentives, call **(800) 962-0973**
or e-mail **premiums@GlobePequot.com.**

First published in 2011 by Quadrille Publishing Limited

First published in the United States in 2012 by Lyons Press

Text © 2011 Niamh Shields
Photography © 2011 Georgia Glynn Smith
Design and layout © 2011 Quadrille Publishing Limited

Lyons Press is an imprint of Globe Pequot Press.

Library of Congress Cataloging-in-Publication Data is available on file.

ISBN 978-0-7627-8021-1

Printed in China

10 9 8 7 6 5 4 3 2 1

✦ CONTENTS ✦

I love to eat and I love to cook. It gives me very great pleasure. Food doesn't need to be complicated, nor does it need to be fussy. Recipes can take hours, or they can take minutes, the end result can always be wonderful food.

I love to cook for myself, my family, and friends. I love seeing their faces light up when they sample something delicious that I have prepared for them … then I force them to take the recipe home and try it for themselves. My friends' weeks are now littered with instances of my shrimp curry and meatballs, among other things, and this makes me very happy. Cooking really isn't tough!

"But you must be a chef? I can't do that." I'm not! I am an enthusiastic home cook. And, better yet, I'm predominantly self-taught, so really you can do it, too. Go to your butcher, buy some brisket, and slow cook it. Get some squid from your fishmonger —and ask him to prepare it, too—for a weeknight supper. Embrace life and embrace your kitchen. We would all be so much better for it if we did!

I adore spices and flavor, comfort and fun, food that zings and sizzles. Quick weekday recipes and long weekend ones, where my oven does the work while I drink some wine, or often while I sleep.

Simple inexpensive food comes to life with a little bit of attention from some appropriate fresh spices. "Oh, but I hate spicy food." I promise you, you don't. Spices don't always mean heat, they mean flavor. Treat your spice box as a paint palette and watch your food come to life. With a $20 investment in fresh spices every six months, you can change the way you eat and the way you cook.

Slow cooking makes tough meat supple, yielding, and far more delicious than those more expensive cuts. Leftovers from the weekends make weekday evenings quick, simple, and a joy.

So this book is for all of you who are maybe afraid to cook. It's also for those of you who love spending time in your kitchen and are interested in learning about different ways of cooking and expanding your repertoire. I hope you like it.

How to be a better cook

So, you love to cook but want to be better. What should you do?

Shop clever

Choose your produce well. The best food comes from the very best ingredients. Poor ingredients will produce a poor result, even when the very best chef is cooking them.

Always use free-range eggs; organic if possible. I use large free-range organic eggs, which have larger, more flavorful egg yolks. The flavor is far superior, and they cook better and are not full of chemical garbage, as the chickens haven't been pumped with antibiotics or other chemicals.

Always use unwaxed lemons; you wouldn't shave a candle into your dinner now would you? They have much better flavor too.

Eat seasonally, when ingredients are at their best and much cheaper.

Buy from independent retailers. They are often cheaper, the produce is almost always better, they know their product very well, and they can give you great advice on what to do with it.

In the kitchen

Teach yourself the basics; those building blocks will make a huge difference both to your cooking and to your confidence.

Make homemade stock; it takes time not energy and is a great use of those vegetables that are lingering in your refrigerator.

Trust your nose and palate and learn to understand balance in food. If it needs to be sweeter, add some sugar or honey; sour, add some vinegar, tamarind, or sumac; salty, add some salt!

Don't be afraid of fat and salt. In moderation they are fine and they taste good, too.

Big flavors

Add flavor where you can; it makes a big difference. The gentle aroma of a bay leaf can change a soup, some simple spices can make a roast.

Use sea salt and freshly ground pepper. They will enhance your dish.

Play around with salt; it's fun and it makes your cooking interesting! Salt goes with everything. Two of my favorites are ham salt and rosemary salt. They are fun, different, and packed with flavor.

This is so good on eggs or sprinkled on asparagus. Subtle but absolutely delicious, it beats truffle salt hands down any day and is so much cheaper. It's easy too.

Ham salt

Makes about 6 ounces
6 slices prosciutto or jamón Serrano, as thin as possible
5 ounces sea salt

Preheat your oven to 300°F.

Place your ham slices on some wax paper and cook gently until completely crisp but not burned; this will take about 15 minutes. Don't use any oil; they need to be as dry as possible.

Let cool on a wire tray and, when cold, crumble between your fingers until like a powder.

Mix with the sea salt and store in the refrigerator.

This is lovely with lamb or pork and is a quick and easy way of jazzing up a simple piece of meat. It's great with white beans, too.

Rosemary salt

Makes about 5 ounces
5 sprigs of rosemary
5 ounces sea salt

Chop the rosemary needles as finely as you can and mix in with the salt. Store in the refrigerator.

Experiment
Play and enjoy. You won't regret it. You will learn a lot, too.

Most importantly, have fun and don't forget to enjoy eating the fruits of your labors.

Brunch

Cozy weekend brunches for two

I love brunch. It is my favorite and most perfect meal of the week. After rushing around from Monday to Friday, grabbing a bite of breakfast as I head for the door, it's a weekend luxury. Feet up with a big pot of coffee, the papers, sparkling water, and juice. You should eat it in your PJs to make the picture complete. None of these recipes will demand too much of you, but they will all taste great.

There are many reasons to make homemade yogurt. It's simple, it's natural, it's cheap, and it tastes better. You just need a starter (plain yogurt) and some milk (to convert to yogurt) and some time. The end result is yogurt that is sweeter and nicer than any you can buy. Ideally you let it ferment in a Thermos flask, although at room temperature is fine, too (it just may take a little longer). I like to use Jersey or Guernsey milk for this, as the richer the milk, the better the flavor. I love it for a quick breakfast or brunch with a simple fruit compote. Use honey or sugar, whichever you prefer.

Homemade yogurt with rhubarb compote

Serves 6 (but obviously you can keep some for later in the week!)
For the yogurt
4 cups whole milk
¼ cup plain yogurt

For the rhubarb compote
14 ounces rhubarb
up to ¼ cup, plus 2 tablespoons brown sugar (depending on how tart
   your rhubarb is)
juice of 1 orange

The night before, bring the milk to a simmer and turn off the heat. Let the temperature drop to 104°F. You can check the temperature with a thermometer, or just put your finger in: if it's just that little bit too hot, then you're there.

Add the yogurt and stir. Seal in a Thermos, or covered and at room temperature, for seven or eight hours. When the yogurt is ready, the milk will have thickened and formed lumps. This is fine and what you expect. Whisk thoroughly and refrigerate to prevent it from culturing further and becoming too sour.

For your compote, put the rhubarb, sugar, orange juice, and 1 tablespoon of water into a pan and bring to a boil. Reduce the heat and cook for five minutes, until the rhubarb comes apart at the touch of a fork. Stir, let cool, and store in the refrigerator in an airtight jar. Serve on top of your lovely homemade yogurt.

Homemade oatmeal, made using good natural oats (not the quick oats that you can get now), is a perfect start to the day. Using whole milk it is rich and creamy, not the insipid, thick mass most of us associate with our childhood. It is even better if you soak the oats the night before. Apple and cinnamon is a lovely combination, especially with a little honey to sweeten. With regard to the oats, my preference is Irish … but that shouldn't surprise you very much!

Apple and cinnamon oatmeal

Serves 1
½ cup rolled oats
1 heaping cup whole milk
1 baking apple, peeled and chopped into small dice
1 cinnamon stick
honey, to serve

Put the oats into a bowl and stir in the milk. Cover and leave in the refrigerator overnight.

In the morning, tip the oats and milk into a saucepan. Bring to just before a boil with the apple and cinnamon stick, then reduce the heat to low and cook gently, stirring occasionally to ensure that the oatmeal doesn't stick, for 10 minutes.

When the apple is cooked and the oatmeal is lovely and soft, add honey to taste, and eat while hot.

The beginning of the asparagus season is one of the most exciting times of the year for me. It is a glorious vegetable, whether you are using the small frail sprue or thick sturdy stalks. Very fresh asparagus is best and sweetest, as the sugars in this vegetable break down into starch quite quickly. For this recipe, use stalks that are reasonably thick and will stay sturdy and tall. The simplicity and quickness of this is its secret. You want the asparagus to retain some crispness, and the egg yolks to be perfectly soft. Asparagus loves eggs, ham loves eggs, asparagus loves ham ... this is one of those love-in dishes, where each bite will be delicious, and you will mourn each one.

This may seem like a small detail, but do ensure your eggs are at room temperature before you cook them or they will likely crack. In fact I always keep them at room temperature. They don't need to be kept chilled and egg shells are porous and will absorb other flavors in the refrigerator. They keep perfectly well in a dark cupboard at room temperature. You won't need to salt your eggs as the ham is already quite salty.

Asparagus and ham soldiers with eggs

Serves 2
12 asparagus spears
12 slices cured ham (prosciutto, jamón, or similar)
4 eggs

Trim the woody ends of the asparagus spears (bend them until they snap naturally in the right place).

Blanch the asparagus spears in boiling water for two minutes, until starting to soften. Run under cold water until the asparagus is cold and has therefore stopped cooking. Dry the asparagus well and wrap each spear in a slice of ham.

Soft-boil each egg in simmering water for four minutes. Meanwhile, griddle or fry each asparagus spear until the ham crisps on either side.

Slice the tops from the eggs and dip the crispy spears into the yolk. And repeat. Delicious!

✦ PASSION ✦

Lemon and ricotta pancakes with raspberries

These fluffy, sweet pancakes are a delight. They are super-easy to make and extra special if you use Homemade Ricotta (see page 70). It may seem a chore to separate eggs, but it makes a very big difference, I promise. If you have a mixer this recipe is really quick, but it's not too taxing by hand either. Think of the pancakes at the end! If raspberries are out of season, substitute with another fruit. The consistency of these pancakes will depend on how much water is in your ricotta, so drain it for half an hour if you can (homemade is best, as always). For perfectly round pancakes you may want to use a mold, but I make mine freeform and sloppy…
they still taste great.

Serves 2 (3 pancakes each)
3 eggs, separated
2 tablespoons unsalted butter, melted
¼ cup superfine sugar
finely grated zest of 1 unwaxed lemon, and juice of ½
1 heaping cup ricotta cheese (homemade is best, see page 70)
pinch of sea salt
¾ cup all-purpose flour, sifted
½ teaspoon baking powder
light flavorless oil, such as sunflower, to fry
scant 1 cup raspberries
honey, to serve

Whisk the egg yolks, butter, sugar, and lemon zest until fluffy. Whisk in the ricotta, lemon juice, salt, flour, and baking powder.

Separately, whisk the egg whites until they start to form peaks. Gently fold them into the batter, taking care not to knock out the air (the air is the fluffiness).

Heat a little oil in a frying pan placed over medium-high heat. Pour one-sixth of the batter into the hot pan and, when bubbles start appearing, flip. Cook for about two to three minutes longer. Remove from the pan and keep warm while you cook the rest.

Serve in stacks with the raspberries and honey.

The Antipodeans are responsible for me loving this recipe … I have many Antipodean friends in London and frequently visit Antipodean cafes as they have some of the best coffee. It is here that I discovered Bircher muesli. A healthy, flavorful joy it is, too. (Though I should add that the original was developed many years ago by a Swiss doctor, Maximilian Oskar Bircher-Benner!) It's basically oats soaked in water or milk, with grated apple and other fruits and nuts. This is perfect for me as I can't bear raisins and especially hate them in my morning muesli. This is a great alternative. Extra chopped fruit is a delicious and healthy addition.

Bircher muesli

Serves 2
½ cup rolled oats
⅔ cup whole milk
1 large tart dessert apple (Granny Smith or similar), grated
5 tablespoons yogurt (homemade is best, see page 12)
honey, to taste
seasonal chopped fruit (optional)
2 tablespoons coarsely chopped nuts (I like hazelnuts or almonds)

Soak the oats in the milk for a minimum of 10 minutes, but ideally overnight, covered, in the refrigerator.

Add the apple and yogurt and stir through. Add honey to taste.
Serve in bowls with the seasonal fruit, if using, and the nuts on top.

I first made these really simple potato pancakes when in school. It's a traditional Irish dish and a great use of leftover potatoes. It is not to be confused with boxty, another Irish potato cake, which contains grated raw potato. Smoked salmon is a wonderful breakfast fish, especially when it's a good one. My favorite comes from East Cork, where artisan smoker Frank Hederman produces the most wonderful fish smoked over beech wood. Cucumber pickle is a perfect side dish, with just a touch of sugar.

Smoked salmon with potato pancakes and cucumber relish

Serves 2

For the cucumber relish
1 heaping cup cider vinegar
1 cup superfine sugar
1 teaspoon salt
2 cucumbers, sliced as finely as you can

For the pancakes
2 tablespoons unsalted butter, melted, plus more to fry
¼ cup all-purpose flour, sifted, plus more to dust
2 green onions, shredded

1 pound warm mashed potatoes (with no butter or milk added)
sea salt
freshly ground black pepper
1 egg
1 teaspoon light oil, such as sunflower

For the smoked salmon
7 ounces smoked salmon, thinly sliced

For the relish, heat the vinegar, sugar, and salt just until the sugar and salt are dissolved. Let cool. Pour over the cucumbers and leave overnight in the refrigerator (or for at least five hours).

To make the pancakes, add the melted butter, flour, and green onions to the mashed potatoes with a pinch of salt and pepper to taste. Stir with a wooden spoon, adding the egg until it forms a dough.

Knead lightly on a floured work surface, then roll until about ¼ inch thick. Traditionally, the dough is rolled into a circle and cut into triangles, but you can cut it into circles with a cookie cutter or the top of a glass if you prefer.

Fry the pancakes in the oil and a little more butter over medium heat for a couple of minutes on each side, until brown.

Serve with the smoked salmon and cucumber relish.

✦ PASSION ✦

Homemade butter

Homemade butter is a joy to make, even better to eat, and so very easy. Why bother? Because you can choose the best cream and make any butter you like. I love rich yellow creams such as Jersey or Guernsey that give a beautiful, intense, and creamy butter. Use the best cream you can get. You can keep it unsalted (but use it quickly!), or be creative. Make it with sea salt or, for an extra oomph, with smoked or flavored sea salt. Your friends will be really impressed, I promise! You can even get them to make it.

You can make it simply by putting the cream in a jar and shaking it like crazy until the milk separates from the butter or, my preference, just stick it in a mixer and whip it. The first pass will still be quite milky and, if you leave it like this, it will sour pretty quickly, so squeeze and drain it to get the excess moisture out.

Makes about 1¼ cups
1½ cups heavy cream, preferably Jersey cream

Whisk the heavy cream in a mixer, by hand, or in a jar, until the buttermilk separates from the butter fat. Squeeze the solids with your hands to remove excess liquid and whisk or shake it again. Wrap in cheesecloth and hang it over the kitchen sink from your faucet for an hour or so. Use immediately, or store in the refrigerator.

Rose petal butter

This butter is beautiful and fragrant, creamy and sweet, a pretty and delicious start to a weekend or special morning. I love it with pancakes or scones.

Makes 9 ounces
1⅛ cups butter (homemade is best, see above)
petals from 1 organic rose, color of your choice

With the butter at room temperature, cream it until nice and soft, then gently stir in the rose petals until there are swirls of them throughout. Use immediately or wrap and store in the refrigerator for a few days.

These fluffy pancakes will make you smile. The crisp, salty bacon with the sweet, soft, bouncy pancakes is a wondrous combination. The maple syrup is that added extra, the bit that almost pushes the dish too far, but makes it perfect. And delicious.

American-style pancakes with bacon and maple syrup

Serves 1; multiply as required
¾ cup all-purpose flour
1 heaping teaspoon baking powder
1 egg, separated
generous pinch of sea salt
1 teaspoon brown sugar
⅓ cup whole milk
bacon, and as much as you want to eat.
   Three slices for one is a good start!
unsalted butter, to fry
maple syrup, to serve

Sift the flour and baking powder. This is important as the sifting introduces air and will make your pancakes fluffy instead of leaden. Whisk the egg white until it stiffens and forms soft peaks.

Add the salt and sugar to the flour mixture and create a well in the middle. Pour in the egg yolk and the milk. Stir until you get a batter which has no lumps. Fold in the egg white gently, taking care not to knock out the air you've introduced.

Broil the bacon and keep it in a warm oven while you cook the pancakes.

Heat a frying pan over medium-high heat. Melt 2 tablespoons of butter and add a ladleful of pancake batter. Drop from a few inches above and it will spread to form a circular pancake, or close enough to one.

The pancakes will cook quite quickly. As soon as you see bubbles in the batter they are ready to flip. They cook quickly on the other side too and will need just a minute or so. Take a peek; if browned, they're done.

Keep warm in the oven with the bacon while you cook the rest of the pancakes, adding each pancake to the oven as they cook.

To serve, stack the pancakes with bacon in between and on top. Drizzle the maple syrup over to taste. And you're done.

I love this dish, a cheeky take on Mexican huevos rancheros (eggs on tortillas with spicy salsa). In this I substitute potatoes (of course!), resulting in a super-low effort and tasty dish. Good canned tomatoes are great quality and, outside of tomato season, are better than the fresh tomatoes in the stores, so don't feel bad about using them; you will get the best results. Try San Marzano tomatoes or lovely canned pomodorini. They can be expensive, but they are worth it. The only thing to remember is that they are often a little acidic, so some sugar is best added to counter that.

Brunch baked eggs, aka Irish huevos rancheros

Serves 2
1 red onion, minced
1 tablespoon light oil, plus more for the pan
2 garlic cloves, minced
1 red chili, minced (deseeded if you
    don't like things too hot)
14-ounce can good-quality tomatoes
1 teaspoon superfine sugar
sea salt
freshly ground black pepper
9 ounces potatoes (leftover or boiled until tender),
    in chunks
handful of cilantro leaves, chopped
4 eggs

Preheat the oven to 350°F.

Make a quick tomato sauce by sautéing the onion in the oil for five minutes over medium heat until translucent but not brown. Add the garlic and chili for 30 seconds, then add the tomatoes and sugar. Cook for 15 minutes and season to taste.

Put the potatoes into a lightly oiled roasting pan, add the sauce, and roast for 10 minutes. Sprinkle half the cilantro on top and make four spaces for the eggs.

Crack the eggs in and cook for up to five minutes, until the whites are set. The yolks will be starting to set too, but should be still soft. Serve with the rest of the cilantro sprinkled on top.

The perfect breakfast bread: quick, fluffy, and delicious, with the minimum of work. No rising is required and they're ready in five minutes.

Irish soda farls

Serves 2

1⅔ cups all-purpose flour, plus more to dust
½ teaspoon salt
1 teaspoon baking soda
⅔ cup buttermilk

Sift the flour, salt, and baking soda into a bowl. Create a well in the center and add the buttermilk gradually, until the dough holds together but is not too wet. Knead briefly (half a minute or so) on a lightly floured surface. Shape into a circle about ½ inch thick. Divide into eight wedges. Heat a frying pan, add a little flour, and cook the farls on each side over medium heat for eight minutes, turning, until golden brown.

Hash was brought to Boston by the Irish on the famine ships. Leftover potatoes are best, they taste much better fried the next day. I don't know why. I make many types of hash with what I have available, but this is a favorite. Poach or fry the eggs; it's up to you.

Chorizo, potato, and egg hash

Serves 1

7 ounces leftover boiled potatoes, chopped into ½-inch dice
1 teaspoon light oil, such as sunflower or light olive oil
2 cooking chorizo sausages, chopped into ½-inch circles
1 piquillo pepper, or 1 red bell pepper, diced
2 eggs
handful of flat-leaf parsley, chopped

Sauté the potatoes in a large frying pan over medium heat in the oil, stirring to make sure they brown all over. Set aside. In the same pan, sauté the chorizo and pepper for five minutes, until the chorizo starts to crisp and the pepper is soft. If you are poaching eggs, do so now. Return the potatoes to the pan and stir in the parsley.

Create some space for the eggs if you are frying them, and crack them in. Cook until the white is set but the yolk is still runny. Eat hot.

I adore blood sausage, especially Irish blood sausage, which is often wholesome with oats and warm with gentle spicing. I like to roast it until it almost bursts and eat it with runny eggs. I also like croquettes, which are so crispy and delicious they are impossible to resist. Use fresh bread crumbs or Japanese panko. I use panko, as I love the texture and they are so convenient. The croquettes are best fried, but you can bake them too. Tomato goes brilliantly with earthy, rich blood sausage; the fruity sweetness lightens the intensity. Use the best tomatoes you can get, small tomatoes on the vine roasted until almost bursting with a drizzle of olive oil and a sprinkle of sea salt are perfect.

Blood sausage croquettes and roast tomatoes with poached eggs

Serves 1
2 branches of small tomatoes on the vine
    (about 8 tomatoes to a branch)
extra virgin olive oil
sea salt
freshly ground black pepper
2 eggs

For the croquettes
¾ cup all-purpose flour
1 egg
2 cups bread crumbs, or panko crumbs
10 ounces blood sausage, in 1-inch chunks
light oil (peanut or sunflower), to deep-fry

Preheat the oven to 350°F. Put the tomatoes in a roasting pan, drizzle with oil, sprinkle with salt, and roast for 10 minutes.

Meanwhile, arrange on your work surface three shallow bowls. Put the flour in the first bowl and season it well. Beat the egg in the second bowl. Tip the bread crumbs into the third. Coat the blood sausage first in the flour, then the egg, then the bread crumbs.

It is best to fry for flavor and texture, either in a deep-fryer, or fill a deep pan with 2 inches of oil. Place over medium-high heat. When a piece of bread fizzes and crisps in the oil immediately, it is ready. Fry the croquettes until brown and crispy. Drain on paper towels.

While the croquettes are frying, prepare your eggs (either poached or fried). And you're done. Enjoy your lovely brunch.

Homebaked beans are another simple luxury. I cook up a huge pan of beans and freeze them in 2-cup batches (the equivalent, roughly, of a can of beans) so I can prepare great bean dishes super-quickly. They really are superior in taste and texture. I find canned beans can be soggy and tasteless. This is worth the effort as it's fresh and spritely and will liven up your breakfast. It keeps well for a few days in the refrigerator, too. It has a tomato base, some chili, and some summer zucchini to give it a spring in its step. You can prepare it in 30 minutes on a summer weekend morning.

Homebaked beans with zucchini and chili

Serves 2

1 red onion, minced
1 tablespoon olive oil
2 zucchini, quartered lengthwise and chopped
2 garlic cloves, minced
1 red chili, minced (deseeded if you don't like too much heat)
2 cups cooked navy, cannellini, or other white beans (homecooked are best, see page 160), or 14-ounce can white beans, drained and rinsed
1 heaping cup light vegetable or chicken stock
14-ounce can tomatoes
1 teaspoon superfine sugar
1 tablespoon balsamic vinegar
sea salt
freshly ground black pepper
handful of basil leaves

Sauté the onion in the olive oil over medium heat for five minutes, until translucent. Add the zucchini for three minutes or so, until they start to lose some of their water. Add the garlic and chili for 30 seconds, then add the beans, stock, tomatoes, sugar, and balsamic vinegar.

Cook for 10 minutes and season to taste. Shred the basil and stir through just before serving.

I live a mile from one of the most Turkish streets in London, so I am no stranger to these eggs. They are so simple and surprisingly delicious. The first time I saw them, I knew I just had to try: yogurt, spiced melted butter, and poached eggs. Whatever would that taste like? Great!

Don't be afraid of poached eggs; there is no secret. Well, if there is it is simply that your eggs need to be as fresh as possible. A fresh egg has a tight white and it will pull around the yolk when you poach it. Eggs in the store are usually already a week old, so buy them on the day you'll use them, or better still in the farmers' market, if you can. I do the whirlpool technique which I was taught. It may seem excessive, but I love a good poached egg. If I am making more than one, I chill the poached eggs in ice water ready to reheat in hot water for 30 seconds when they are all ready. Some people add vinegar, which helps keep the white tight, but if the eggs are fresh this isn't necessary. Whatever works for you. There is a lot of butter in this; do feel free to scale back. You won't regret it if you don't, though. There are three ways to flavor these: you can go with spice (paprika); or with aroma (sage); or you can even combine the two. The crispy sage leaves are heavenly in the melted butter; the paprika is wonderful too. Try either and try them together as well. I can never decide which I prefer.

Turkish eggs

Serves 1
2 eggs
2 tablespoons unsalted butter
6 sage leaves, or ½ teaspoon hot paprika, or both
⅓ cup thick Greek yogurt

Poach the eggs. Bring a deep pan of water to a gentle simmer (small bubbles will be rising to the surface, just before a boil).

This is easier to do if you crack each egg into a ramekin or cup so that you can easily drop it into the whirlpool while it's still busy spinning.

Create a little whirlpool by running a spoon around the edges of the simmering water until there is a fast-moving swirl in the center. Drop in your egg and, when the white is firm, it's done. Repeat with the second egg.

While the eggs are poaching, melt the butter. Crisp the sage leaves in the butter, if using, or add the paprika to the melted butter, if using.

Create a pillow of the yogurt in the bottom of a bowl. Put the poached eggs on top and drizzle that lovely melted butter over them. Add the sage leaves too, if using. The crispy leaves make a wonderful contrast to the creamy, rich egg yolk.

Speedy Suppers
Full-flavored quick food for weeknights

Lots of people tell me that they can't eat well during the week as they are too busy and don't have time. I disagree. There is always half an hour that can be clawed back and dragged to the kitchen for the sake of a quick, delicious, nutritious meal. Some of these dishes take longer than that to cook, but the prep is quick for most, which means that while they are cooking you can go about your normal everyday busy business. Reclaim your evening suppers!

Halloumi is a great Mediterranean cheese easily found in Greek or Turkish stores. It doesn't melt well and so is ideal for frying. It's a perfect thing to serve to vegetarian friends. Very salty, it is lovely in this salad, offset with fruity tomatoes and pomegranate seeds. I add onion for texture and parsley gives it a lift. The dressing is simple and fruity, just pomegranate molasses and olive oil with a tiny bit of red wine vinegar. Some pomegranate molasses can be quite sour and, if yours is, you may not need the vinegar, so taste it before using. It's a killer ingredient. As a dressing or marinade it's a best friend to lamb and chicken as well. I had to refrain from using it in too many recipes in this book!

Halloumi and pomegranate salad

Serves 2

2 tablespoons pomegranate molasses
2 tablespoons extra virgin olive oil
1 tablespoon red wine vinegar
sea salt
freshly ground black pepper
½ red onion, thinly sliced
12 cherry tomatoes, halved
9 ounces block halloumi, cut into ¼-inch slices
1 teaspoon light olive oil
seeds of ½ pomegranate
handful of flat-leaf parsley, chopped

Make the dressing by combining the pomegranate molasses, extra virgin olive oil, and vinegar and stirring thoroughly. Season to taste.

Arrange the red onion slices and tomatoes on two plates.

Lightly fry the halloumi—ideally in a griddle pan to get those lovely dark stripes—in the light olive oil on both sides, for a minute or so each, until brown. Place on top of the onion and tomatoes.

Drizzle with the dressing and scatter with the pomegranate seeds and parsley. Eat at once.

This is a great quick meal but, better still, the leftovers make a great lunch. If you're not a fan of chickpeas, feel free to substitute with cooked white beans. Fresh spices, as I reiterate so often in this book, make all the difference. Roasting and grinding your own spices only takes seconds and I strongly recommend you do it. I find sharp feta cheese goes well with gentle, soothing spinach and spicy beans. Serve with toasted pita bread.

Spiced chickpea, spinach, and feta salad

Serves 2
1 teaspoon coriander seeds
1 teaspoon cumin seeds
½ teaspoon turmeric
½ teaspoon chili powder
½ teaspoon garam masala
1 small onion, minced
1 celery stalk, finely sliced
1 tablespoon light oil, such as sunflower or peanut
1-inch chunk fresh gingerroot, grated
1 fat garlic clove, minced
4 ounces cherry or baby plum tomatoes, quartered
2 cups cooked chickpeas (homecooked are best, see page 160),
    or 14-ounce can chickpeas, drained and rinsed
couple of handfuls of spinach
handful of cilantro leaves, chopped
7 ounces feta cheese, crumbled
sea salt
freshly ground black pepper
juice of ½ unwaxed lemon

Toast the coriander and cumin seeds in a dry frying pan until they start to pop; no more than one minute. Grind the toasted seeds in a mortar and pestle. Combine with the turmeric, chili powder, and garam masala.

Fry the onion and celery in the oil until the onion is translucent, then add the spices, ginger, and garlic and fry for a minute or so. Add the tomatoes and cook for a couple of minutes. Add the chickpeas and coat in the spices. Add the spinach and stir until wilted. Take off the heat and stir in the cilantro and feta. Season and add lemon juice to taste. The lemon juice lifts the flavors and gives a lovely freshness.

I came across the idea for this recipe when investigating Chinese New Year recipes. These are called "long life noodles" in China. I love eating for an occasion, even when it is not culturally my own! The idea is that you don't cut or break the noodles as it is very bad luck for your own lifespan. (Although I am sure you'll be OK if you do.)

Tofu is a much underrated ingredient; it carries the flavors of whatever you put with it and is solid protein. It is particularly good with the tannic green tea and sweet red pepper here. Asian—and particularly Japanese—grocery stores serve terrific fresh tofu, so do investigate there if you can. Most grocery stores do now, too. Go for the packages in the refrigerator over those on the shelf.

This dish tastes great hot or cold. Leftovers are very good for lunch the next day.

Chinese noodles with tofu and green tea

Serves 2

7 ounces medium egg or udon noodles
2 tablespoons light oil, such as sunflower or peanut
1 teaspoon green tea leaves, preferably gunpowder
1-inch chunk fresh gingerroot, minced
2 garlic cloves, minced
1 large red bell pepper, cut into thin strips
7 ounces firm tofu, cut into thin sticks
4 green onions, cut diagonally into 1-inch pieces
2 tablespoons soy sauce
2 tablespoons rice vinegar
1 teaspoon toasted sesame oil
sea salt
freshly ground black pepper

Bring a large pot of water to a boil. Cook the noodles according to the package instructions. Drain and rinse with cold water to stop them from cooking. Set aside.

Heat the oil in a frying pan or wok over medium heat. Add the tea leaves, ginger, and garlic and cook for about 30 seconds. Add the red bell pepper and tofu, stirring gently until the peppers begin to soften. Add the noodles and cook for a couple of minutes, stirring gently until the noodles are warmed through.

Add the green onions, soy sauce, rice vinegar, and sesame oil. Season to taste and serve.

Lentil soup, harissa croutons

A gentle, smooth red lentil soup is a perfect carrier for spicy, crisp harissa croutons. I love playing with croutons. They are receptive to so many flavors. These harissa croutons are great—spicy and crispy—though a mellow crouton of good bread tossed in Parmesan, parsley, and olive oil is terrific in salad. There's so much scope.

Serves 4

1 tablespoon harissa (homemade is best, see below)
3 tablespoons extra virgin olive oil
sea salt
freshly ground black pepper
4 ounces leftover good bread, cubed
1 tablespoon cumin seeds
1 banana shallot, minced
1 tablespoon light oil, such as sunflower
1 mild green chili, minced
1 garlic clove, minced
5 cups light vegetable or chicken stock
½ cup red lentils
7 ounces baby spinach
squeeze of lemon

Preheat the oven to 300°F. Combine the harissa and olive oil and season. Toss with the bread to coat. Bake for 20–25 minutes, until crisp, shaking occasionally. Meanwhile, place the cumin seeds in a small dry frying pan over medium heat and stir until aromatic. Grind to a powder in a mortar and pestle.

Sauté the shallot in the oil over medium heat for five minutes, until translucent. Add the cumin, chili, and garlic and cook for 30 seconds. Pour in the stock and lentils; cook for 10–15 minutes, until the lentils break down. Pack in the spinach, stir to wilt, and turn off the heat. Squeeze over lemon, season, and serve with the spicy croutons.

Tip: to make **homemade harissa**, roast a red bell pepper over a gas flame until black all over. Place in a plastic storage bag and let cool. Blend with 4 red chilies, deseeded, 1 tablespoon toasted and ground cumin seeds, 2 garlic cloves, chopped, 1 teaspoon red wine vinegar, and 2 tablespoons extra virgin olive oil, and season with sea salt.

This is a heady combination of deep savory flavors, very rich and appetizing. Called *nasu dengaku* in Japan, it is perfect comfort food. It will sooth any stomachache and take away anything that is bothering you when you first bite into it.

I first had this dish on a trip to Japan and subsequently many times in Japanese restaurants in London. Luckily, it is super-easy to make at home, too. A simple trinity of mirin (rice wine), sake, and miso dominate, with sugar to sweeten, savory sesame oil, and seeds. It's perfect with plain white rice, with which you will chase the remaining miso around the plate.

The ingredients are very easy to source; most large grocery stores will have all of these things. There are many types of miso paste, a sweet white variety is best but all will do well. Don't be tempted to substitute packages of miso soup; it won't be very nice! Use good miso for the best results.

Eggplant with miso

Serves 2
1 tablespoon mirin, or light sherry
1 tablespoon sake
1 tablespoon superfine sugar
3 tablespoons miso paste
1 large eggplant, halved lengthwise
1 tablespoon light oil, such as peanut
1 tablespoon sesame seeds

Make the sauce by heating the mirin, sake, and sugar and boiling the alcohol off over a couple of minutes. Reduce the heat and add the miso. Cook gently for a few more minutes.

Slash the eggplant diagonally through the flesh at 1-inch intervals. Put cut side down into a frying pan with the oil over medium heat. Cook on this side for two minutes.

Turn over and cook on the skin side until the eggplant is soft to the touch and a knife goes easily through it. It should take a maximum of five minutes, but will depend on the size of your eggplant.

Heat the broiler and spoon the sauce over each eggplant half. Sprinkle with the sesame seeds and broil until the sauce is bubbling.

Serve immediately with rice.

Tip: the little eggplants that you find in Asian food stores—and increasingly in grocery stores—cooked this way make terrific grazing food for friends.

Any white fish or salmon works really well in fish cakes, but it's hard to beat a good smoked haddock. These are quick and filling, leftovers make great lunch and, if you want to make extra for another night, they freeze really well.

Smoked haddock fish cakes with green salad

Serves 4
For the fish cakes
1 onion
10 cloves
4 cups whole milk
3 bay leaves
14 ounces smoked haddock (preferably undyed)
2 pounds potatoes
handful of flat-leaf parsley, roughly chopped
4 tablespoons unsalted butter (optional), plus more to fry
3 green onions, finely sliced
sea salt

freshly ground black pepper
2 eggs, beaten
¾ cup all-purpose flour
4 cups bread crumbs
olive oil, to fry

For the salad
1 head green lettuce of your choice, separated into leaves
12 cherry tomatoes, halved
2 green onions, minced
juice of ½ unwaxed lemon
2 tablespoons extra virgin olive oil

Halve the onion, peel, and stud with the cloves. Add to the milk and bay leaves in a pan that can fit the fish lying flat. Bring to just below a simmer, reduce the heat, and add the haddock, ensuring it is covered with milk. Let poach gently for 15 minutes or so, ensuring the milk never boils. Let the fish cool and flake gently.

Boil the potatoes until tender, then mash. Add the fish to the potatoes with the parsley, butter, if using, green onion, and some of the poaching milk, if required (only if your mixture is dry; you don't want it sloppy though). Season with salt and pepper. Shape into eight large or 12 smaller balls and flatten until they are no more than ¾ inch thick.

Place the eggs in a shallow bowl, and the flour in a second, seasoning the flour well. Put the bread crumbs on a plate. Coat each fish cake in flour, then in egg, then bread crumbs. If you want more bread crumbs on the cakes, repeat the egg and crumb layers again.

Make your salad by combining all the ingredients and dressing with the lemon and extra virgin olive oil, seasoning to taste.

Shallow-fry the fish cakes in a mixture of olive oil and butter over medium heat for about five minutes on each side, taking care they don't burn. Serve warm with the salad.

This is a great way to liven up some salmon, adding a crunchy texture and making it healthier, too. Sesame seeds are super-healthy and have been shown to have a cholesterol-lowering effect. Could this dish be any healthier? I don't think it could. My favorite almonds are Spanish Marcona: small, round, and delicious, they have a gorgeous flavor, and are a good size. Any almonds will do however. They make a lovely textural contrast with the juicy tomatoes, and this salad to me screams health. Enjoy it and use it to balance out one of your pork days, that's what I do! The quality of the ingredients is important here; a poor balsamic vinegar won't be jammy enough to liven up the tomatoes, while bad tomatoes just taste bad, so get the best you can and enjoy.

Sesame-crusted salmon with tomato and almond salad

Serves 2
For the salmon
1/3 cup sesame seeds
2 x 5-ounce salmon fillets
2 tablespoons olive oil
1 tablespoon light oil

For the salad
1/2 cup almonds, preferably Marcona
7 ounces good tomatoes, in 1/2-inch dice
3 ounces arugula leaves
1 tablespoon good balsamic vinegar
2 tablespoons extra virgin olive oil
sea salt
freshly ground black pepper

Place the sesame seeds in a shallow bowl or on a plate. Coat the salmon in the olive oil and then in the seeds, coating all sides.

Fry the salmon in the light oil over medium heat for six to eight minutes, turning once, until cooked through but still very tender in the middle. Take care not to burn the seeds or overcook the fish.

Meanwhile, toast the almonds quickly in a dry pan. Gently combine with the tomatoes and arugula, then dress with the balsamic and oil. Season to taste.

Serve the fish hot on top of the salad.

I love this recipe and it is one of my most popular that I cook at home. Most of my friends make it all the time now, too. It's so delicious and healthy and packed with flavor. You will definitely want more, so I would recommend making double and packing leftovers for lunch the next day.

I like to serve this curry with brown basmati rice that's been rinsed and cooked with twice its volume of salted water. I frequently add a few cardamom pods, cloves, and cinnamon bark to the rice to flavor it lightly. It complements the cloves in the sauce.

Shrimp curry

Serves 2
1 tablespoon cumin seeds
12 black peppercorns
4 cloves
2 teaspoons ground turmeric
1 onion, minced
1-inch chunk fresh gingerroot, minced or grated
1 green chili (more if you like it spicier)
1 tablespoon light oil
2 garlic cloves, minced
14-ounce can diced tomatoes
1 teaspoon superfine sugar
14-ounce can coconut milk
9 ounces raw shrimp, shelled and deveined
3 tablespoons chopped cilantro leaves
juice of ½ unwaxed lemon
sea salt
freshly ground black pepper

Fry the cumin for a minute in a dry frying pan and grind with the other whole spices in a mortar and pestle or spice grinder. Add the turmeric.

Fry the onion, ginger, and chili in the oil until the onion is soft and translucent. Add the garlic and fry for a couple of minutes. Add the spices and stir for a minute or so to temper them. Add the tomatoes and sugar and cook, stirring, for five minutes. Pour in the coconut milk, bring to a boil, and cook for about 15 minutes, or until reduced by at least one-third. Add the shrimp and cook until pink. It will only take a few minutes; take care not to overcook them.

Add the cilantro and lemon juice to taste, to lift the flavor. Season and serve immediately.

I love calamari for supper. It's so quick, healthy, and delicious. It is easy to source too, cheap, and ethically sound as it's not overfished in any way. I like to use smaller squid that are about six inches long and cut them into rings.

Calamari with tomato and green bean salad

Serves 2
3 tablespoons extra virgin olive oil
1 tablespoon balsamic vinegar
sea salt
freshly ground black pepper
⅔ cup cornmeal
2 squid, cleaned, cut into rings
7 ounces green beans, trimmed
light oil, to deep-fry
9 ounces cherry tomatoes, halved

Make the dressing by combining the olive oil and balsamic vinegar and stirring. Season to taste.

Place the cornmeal in a shallow bowl and season it. Toss the squid in the seasoned cornmeal and set aside.

Blanch the green beans in boiling water for three to four minutes, until starting to soften but still firm. Run under cold water until cold to stop the cooking.

Heat 2 inches of oil in a deep pan or a deep-fryer until it reaches 350°F on an oil thermometer, or a piece of bread froths the oil immediately when added. Fry the squid until starting to brown, no more than a couple of minutes. Drain on paper towels for a minute or so.

Toss the green beans gently with the tomatoes and the dressing. Serve the calamari on top and eat while warm.

Laksa is a fabulous soupy dish, fresh and lively, spiked with spices, aromatic with lemon grass, sour with tamarind, and sweet and fruity with tomatoes. There are many types specific to parts of Malaysia and everyone has their own. This is one I came up with after much experimentation. I like to use salmon or shrimp, although chicken would work too. It is difficult to get wild salmon these days, but farmed organic can work very well.

Salmon laksa

Serves 2

½ ounce tamarind paste
4 ounces rice vermicelli noodles
2 cups light chicken or fish stock
¼ cup sesame oil
1 quantity Laksa Paste (see below)
9 ounces ripe tomatoes, peeled and chopped
14-ounce can coconut milk

9 ounces salmon fillet, skinned, in 1-inch chunks
1 red bell pepper, finely sliced
1 tablespoon fish sauce
2 ounces bean sprouts
handful of mint leaves
4 green onions, finely sliced
1 lime, quartered

A few hours before you eat, dissolve the tamarind in scant 1 cup hot water, breaking it up with a fork. Cook the noodles according to package instructions, then stop the cooking by running under cold water. Set aside. Strain the tamarind liquid into the stock after it has been soaked.

Add the sesame oil to the laksa paste. Heat in a saucepan for a minute or so. Add the tomatoes and stir for five minutes, until it forms a thick paste. Mix in the stock and coconut milk. Bring to a boil and simmer for five minutes. Add the salmon and red bell pepper and simmer for a few minutes, or until the fish is cooked. Season with the fish sauce. Divide the noodles and bean sprouts between two large bowls and ladle in the soup. Top with mint and green onions and serve with lime wedges.

LAKSA PASTE

1 teaspoon coriander seeds
1–2 red chilies, minced
1-inch chunk fresh gingerroot, minced
2 lemon grass stalks, trimmed, halved lengthwise, and minced
3 garlic cloves, minced
handful of cilantro leaves

Toast the coriander seeds in a dry frying pan for a minute. Grind in a mortar and pestle or blender with the chilies, ginger, lemon grass, garlic, and cilantro to form a paste.

Growing up in Ireland, I thought that eating crabs was plain insane. Our elderly neighbor used to catch enormous ones in a bucket at a rocky beach near our house and boil them up for her Alsatian dog. I envy that dog now, but at the time I felt it was an act of cruelty. I was also terrified she would come near me with her bucket of living, sideways-walking friends. I was afraid of crabs, and really anything living in the sea. I remember standing on an isolated rock shrieking with horror as the crabs ascended. I thought that they would eat me. Of course they didn't, but I eat them now.

This is super-simple and a lovely expression of fresh crab. It benefits from the best ingredients, particularly the crab and the pasta. Bronze die pasta has a grainier surface—where the pasta has been extruded through a bronze die rather than the more common nylon—and so is better for clinging to sauces; it is also much more delicious.

Crab linguine with chili, parsley, and lemon

Serves 2
10 ounces linguine
nice fruity extra virgin olive oil
1 red chili, deseeded and minced
5 ounces white crab meat
finely grated zest and juice of ½ unwaxed lemon
handful of flat-leaf parsley, chopped
sea salt
freshly ground black pepper

Cook your linguine according to the package instructions so that it's just shy of al dente (it will cook a little more when you add it to the crab).

Heat about 2 tablespoons of the oil, add the chili, and stir for about 30 seconds. Add the crab and stir until it's nice and hot.

Add the linguine to the crab and chili and stir through, ensuring that the pasta is nicely coated; drizzle with some more oil if it's dry.

Add lemon juice to taste and some lemon zest with the parsley. Season to taste and serve immediately.

This recipe is a traditional Sardinian dish that is like the seaside on your plate. Fregola is a small, hand-shaped Sardinian pasta, which to me look like miniature bronzed pebbles on the beach. It is exceptional with vongole and fruity tomatoes and also very good with fresh cheeses. It's an obscure ingredient but a really good one, so I wanted to include it in my book. It is increasingly available in good Italian delis and is easily sourced online, too. You can substitute with Israeli couscous if you can't get it, or another small pasta shape. Palourde clams are available in fishmongers and good grocery stores.

Fregola Sarda with vongole

Serves 2

1⅓ pounds palourde/carpetshell clams
sea salt
2 garlic cloves, minced
10 ounces baby plum tomatoes, quartered, or large tomatoes,
    peeled, deseeded, and chopped
2 tablespoons extra virgin olive oil
2 cups light stock, such as chicken or vegetable
3 ounces fregola Sarda
handful of flat-leaf parsley, chopped
freshly ground black pepper

Cover the clams with some salted water for 10 minutes, then rinse. This will allow any sand in the shell to come out. Throw away any open clams that don't close when you tap them; these are dead, won't taste good, and will probably make you ill.

While the clams are soaking, sauté the garlic and tomatoes in the oil, in a big pan which has a lid, over medium-low heat for five minutes.

Add the stock and the fregola and cook until the fregola is almost done (this will depend on your fregola, but no more than five minutes).

Add the rinsed clams and cover the pan for two minutes. The clams will have popped open. Discard any that are still closed.

Stir through the parsley. Season to taste and serve immediately.

This is a healthy dish that takes minutes and is full of flavor. Good food that tastes great doesn't have to be torture! I like to use trout as it has a very delicate flavor and is really good with both the avocado in the guacamole and the lime. Trout is very reasonably priced and available virtually everywhere so there is no excuse, really.

Trout with chunky guacamole

Serves 2
For the chunky guacamole
2 ripe avocados
juice of ½ lime
3 green onions, minced
1 green chili, deseeded and minced
1 garlic clove, minced
3 ounces baby plum or cherry tomatoes, quartered
handful of cilantro leaves, chopped
sea salt
freshly ground black pepper

For the fish
1 tablespoon light oil
1 pound 2 ounces trout fillets

Peel and roughly chop the avocados. Add the lime quickly, or the avocado will discolor, then the green onions, chili, and garlic. Mash roughly. Stir in the tomato and cilantro and season to taste.

Heat the oil over medium heat in a frying pan and cook the trout fillets for two minutes on each side, or until done.

Eat immediately with the guacamole.

Gremolata is lively and spritely and often served with a rich beef or veal ragu to lift the meaty intensity (see page 140). It stands up really well on its own, too, as a marinade and is terrific with both pork and chicken. It is really simple and very cheap to make, simply lemon zest (from unwaxed lemons; you don't want wax melting on to your lovely chicken), chopped parsley, and garlic.

This is a favorite speedy supper of mine, marinated and roasted until crisp. Butterflying flattens the chicken, making it much quicker to cook. Marinate the chicken for a couple of hours if you can, or put it in before you go to work and it will be full of flavor by the time you get home. Leftovers make great salad fodder for the next day.

Butterflying a chicken is very easy: just cut out the backbone with poultry shears or a sharp knife and flatten it down, pressing on the breastbone with your palm. You will need to loosen some of the joints to make it completely flat; just jiggle them about a bit! Easier still is to get your butcher to do it for you.

Gremolata butterflied chicken

Serves 2
1 small chicken, butterflied
handful of flat-leaf parsley, chopped
4 garlic cloves, minced
finely grated zest of 1 unwaxed lemon
2 tablespoons extra virgin olive oil
sea salt

Weigh the chicken, so you can calculate its cooking time later.

Combine the parsley, garlic, lemon zest, and olive oil and add a pinch of sea salt. Rub into the butterflied chicken, cover, and let marinate in the refrigerator for two hours (or more) if you can. Don't worry too much if you can't marinate it for too long. It will still taste great.

Preheat the oven to 400°F. Return the chicken to room temperature. Cook for 15 minutes per 1 pound plus 15 minutes more, turning halfway through and finishing breast side up so it gets nice and crispy. Rest for 10 minutes, then serve.

Right now, as I type and you read, there are people all over Lisbon eating rotisserie chickens saturated in piri piri and painting on more with big thick brushes dripping in the marinade. In Lisbon they cook the chickens in a rotisserie after a long rest in the marinade. I don't have a rotisserie at home—I expect you don't either—so I roast mine instead and it is a great dish and a perfect weekend lunch. It's also a brilliant speedy supper when you focus on the thighs and legs of the chicken, as I do here.

Cooking chicken in vinegar is common in many cultures. Chicken in red wine vinegar is served in Lyonnaise bouchons (and it's delicious!). Chicken en escabeche is the Spanish/Mexican equivalent. I love this Portuguese recipe as it is lively with spice.

Piri piri is a chili, also called Thai chili, and very fiery. If it's too hot for you, substitute fewer, milder chilies; it will still taste great. Make life easier by making the marinade the night before and marinating your chicken overnight. It will seep through the skin and permeate the flesh, giving great flavor throughout and keeping it really moist. Then all you've got to do is chuck it in the oven and let it roast. The juices that collect make a terrific sauce; be sure to spoon them over the chicken as you serve it.

Piri piri chicken

Serves 2
2 chicken thighs, skin on
2 chicken legs, skin on

For the marinade
½ cup red wine vinegar
scant ⅓ cup extra virgin olive oil
6 Thai chilies, deseeded and chopped
3 garlic cloves, minced
1 tablespoon thyme leaves

The day before, prick the chicken skin several times with a fork. Mix the ingredients for the marinade and massage it in so the chicken gets to know it! Cover and refrigerate overnight, if possible, for the best flavor.

Supper time: preheat the oven to 350°F. Roast the chicken pieces, skin side up, for 30 minutes and check on them. They will likely need 10 more minutes and will be done when the skin is browning and slightly crisp (the marinade will prevent it getting really crisp, but it is worth the sacrifice). Serve the chicken with the marinade and juices spooned over it.

Tip: this makes a really terrific Sunday roast too, with a whole chicken marinated and roasted.

A herby twist on chicken Milanese, this can be fried or roasted. Fried will give a better crumb and will be marginally fattier. Roasted is still good and should keep your conscience at bay. Sage and lemon are perfect partners. Ensure your sage is finely shredded as it is quite strong. I like to use Japanese panko, a great dry crumb that is now easily available. Any bread crumbs will do though.

Breaded lemon and sage chicken

Serves 2
2 chicken breasts, skinless and boneless
⅓ cup all-purpose flour
sea salt
freshly ground black pepper
1 egg, beaten
1 cup bread crumbs, or panko crumbs
1 tablespoon fresh sage leaves, finely shredded
finely grated zest of 1 unwaxed lemon
¼ cup olive oil (optional)

Flatten the chicken with a meat mallet, if you have one, or a rolling pin, until it's about half as thick as when you started (about ½ inch).

Set out three shallow bowls. Pour the flour into the first and season it well. Put the egg in the second and, in the third, mix the bread crumbs, sage, and lemon zest.

Dip the chicken in the flour, shaking off the excess, then into the egg, letting the excess drip off, and finally coat thoroughly in bread crumbs. Repeat for the second piece of chicken.

To fry, heat the olive oil, if using, until a piece of bread starts to fizz and crisp immediately, then fry the chicken for three minutes or so on each side until brown.

To roast, preheat the oven to 400°F. Place the chicken on an oiled dish and roast for 15–20 minutes, or until cooked through. You can test by cutting through the thickest part of the chicken; it should no longer be pink.

These pies are super, full-flavored, and bursting to get out from under the pastry.
I use cooking chorizo and chicken thighs, as they have the best flavor and stay moist.
I make these in 4¾ x 3-inch cast-iron dishes.

Chicken and chorizo pie

Serves 4
1 tablespoon unsalted butter, plus more for the dishes
1 tablespoon olive oil
1 pound 2 ounces chicken (preferably thigh meat), diced
7 ounces cooking chorizo, sliced
2 fat garlic cloves, minced
1 mild red chili, deseeded and minced
14-ounce can tomatoes
2 teaspoons Spanish paprika
sea salt
freshly ground black pepper
handful of flat-leaf parsley, chopped
9 ounces ready-rolled all-butter puff pastry
1 egg, beaten

Preheat the oven to 350°F. Heat the butter and oil in a large sauté pan or
saucepan over medium heat, and sauté the chicken until it starts to
brown. Remove the chicken and sauté the chorizo for a few minutes
until it starts to release oil, then add the garlic and chili for a minute or
so, stirring to ensure it doesn't burn.

Add the tomatoes and paprika, return the chicken, and bring to a
boil. Reduce the heat to low and simmer for 10 minutes. Season to taste.
Remove from the heat and stir in the parsley.

Cut lids from the pastry to fit each pie dish, using a dish as a guide.
Butter each pie dish and divide the pie filling between each. Add the
pastry lids, brush with the egg, and cook for 20 minutes or so, or until
delightfully crisp and brown.

Duck breast is a completely different meat than duck leg. Duck leg is best cooked until falling off the bone and is rich and juicy with fat (see right), while duck breast is perfect and delicate when cooked only until still rosy and pink. It takes no time to cook and is delicious with fruit (plums or cherries), herbs, and spices (five spice, star anise, or chili). This recipe calls for a marinade and, as with all marinades, the longer you marinate the more you will benefit. Aim for two hours if you can.

Soy and spice duck breast

Serves 2
5 tablespoons soy sauce
¼ cup rice wine
2 tablespoons honey
2 star anise
1 red chili, minced
2 garlic cloves, minced
1-inch chunk fresh gingeroot, minced
3 cloves
1 large cinnamon stick, broken in pieces
sea salt
freshly ground black pepper
2 duck breasts, rinsed and wiped dry

Mix all the ingredients except the duck breasts and season to taste. Bash them with a rolling pin or pestle to get the flavors talking to each other. Slash the duck breast through the skin at ½-inch intervals, but not through the fat. Pour some boiling water over the skin and pat dry. This will allow some of the fat to run off.

Cover the duck with the marinade in a compact dish or a freezer bag and rub it in with your fingers. Cover and marinate in the refrigerator for as long as possible, at least two hours if you can, or overnight.

Wipe the marinade from the duck breasts and fry in a dry frying pan over low to medium heat, skin side down, for eight to 10 minutes, to render most of the fat and crisp the skin. No oil is necessary; there's lots of fat in the duck already.

When the skin is crisped slightly, turn over and increase the heat to medium. Cook for another five minutes or so, until the breast meat is light pink but cooked. Let rest for a couple of minutes.

Serve sliced on top of stir-fried pak choi, or noodles fried with sesame oil, cilantro, and green onion.

I love roast duck legs. Relatively cheap and quick to roast, they are a perfect quick meal. I like to spice these as I do the breast but the approach is a little simpler, using just chili powder and Chinese five spice.

Roast the duck legs on top of the potatoes so the potatoes absorb all the gorgeous and delicious fat. If you are watching what you eat you may prefer to roast the duck separately, although you will miss a lot of the joy of the dish. This screams comfort and winter, but don't be afraid to spruce it up for summer with a nice salad.

Spiced roast duck legs with potatoes and pancetta

Serves 2
2 duck legs
¼ teaspoon chili powder
½ teaspoon five spice
2 slices pancetta, diced
12 ounces potatoes, diced
handful of flat-leaf parsley leaves, chopped
pinch of sea salt

Preheat the oven to 425°F. Prick the duck legs all over with a fork. Combine the chili powder and five spice and rub into the duck legs. Set aside.

Fry the pancetta in its own fat for a couple of minutes over medium heat, until starting to crisp. Toss with the potatoes and place in a small, high-sided roasting pan with the duck legs on top.

Roast for 10 minutes to crisp the skin, then reduce the oven temperature to 375°F and cook for 40 minutes, when the duck legs should be cooked through. You can check by seeing if the meat is pulling away from the bone.

Remove the duck legs from the roasting tray and add the parsley to the potatoes and pancetta. Season with salt to taste. Let rest for five minutes, then serve the duck legs on top of the potatoes.

Sadly I have never been to Beijing, but I have been to Chinatown and this is where I learned of *jiaozi* or Beijing dumplings. Easy to reproduce at home, they are the most perfect comfort food.

I highly recommend making the wrappers at home—if you have time—with dumpling flour from Asian stores; it makes a difference. However, for a quick weekday meal, ready-made dumpling or wonton wrappers are fine.

Beijing dumplings with chili and soy dipping sauce

Serves 4

For the filling
1 pound ground pork
3 green onions, minced
1 garlic clove, minced
handful of Chinese chives
    (or normal chives), minced
1 tablespoon rice wine vinegar
½ teaspoon sesame oil
sea salt
freshly ground white pepper

For the wrappers
EITHER
1 small package gyoza or wonton wrappers
OR
1¾ cups dumpling flour, or 1⅔ cups all-
    purpose flour mixed with 3 tablespoons
    cornstarch or rice flour, plus more to dust
pinch of salt

For the dip
⅓ cup soy sauce
1 teaspoon chili oil or 1 red chili, minced

Mix the ingredients for the filling, cover, and leave in the refrigerator while you make the wrappers. This will allow the flavors to integrate.

For the wrappers, combine the flour or flours, salt, and 5 tablespoons of water and mix. Knead for 10 minutes, until shiny and elastic, or put in your mixer and let it do the work for five minutes. You may want to add more water or flour; you want a mixture that is firm without being too wet. Cover in cling wrap or put in a plastic storage bag for 30 minutes in the refrigerator.

Pull off little balls, smaller than a quarter coin, and roll on a floured work surface until as thin as you can get without tearing, each about 3 inches in diameter. Mix together the ingredients for the dipping sauce.

Brush the edges of the wrappers lightly with water (not too much or they'll get soggy). Place a teaspoon of filling in the center, fold in a half moon shape, and press or pleat closed, ensuring they are sealed.

Steam in a steamer or bamboo steaming basket for 15-20 minutes, or until tender and cooked through. Otherwise, add to boiling water for a few minutes; they will be cooked two minutes after they float to the top. Serve hot with the dipping sauce.

We need to see more pork burgers and I can never have enough chorizo in my life, so I came up with the recipe for these lively patties. They are perfect eaten in crispy pita breads with a little salad or in a Middle Eastern khobez flatbread. Simple, quick, delicious, what more do you need in a quick dinner? Answers on a postcard please.

Pork and chorizo burgers

Makes 4

For the burgers
3 ounces cooking chorizo
1 garlic clove, minced
handful of flat-leaf parsley, chopped
14 ounces ground pork
sea salt
freshly ground black pepper
1 tablespoon light oil

To serve
small pita breads (or a wrap, bun, or similar)
mayonnaise (homemade is best, see page 75)
arugula leaves, or similar salad green
chopped tomatoes (I use juicy small tomatoes)

Peel the skin from the chorizo and chop as finely as you can. Add the garlic, parsley, and chorizo to the pork and mix thoroughly. Season with salt and pepper. Cook a small amount in a frying pan and eat to check the seasoning; adjust if necessary. Shape the mixture into four patties.

If you have a griddle, heat it until it's extremely hot. Otherwise use a frying pan. There's lots of fat in the pork so you won't need much oil. Fry on one side for four to five minutes and turn. Reduce the heat slightly and let the burger cook through. It should take up to 10 minutes. Check by cutting into one: if it's pink, it's not ready.

Serve in toasted pita breads (or your bread of choice), with some mayonnaise, arugula, and tomatoes.

I love sumac, a gorgeous Middle Eastern spice made from ground berries. Sour in flavor, it is especially terrific with lamb. It wakes up these sleepy little meatballs, cozy in their cinnamon tomato sauce, while the cumin gives a robust background flavor. Sumac is relatively easy to source these days, but if you are struggling it is easily available online. For a super-speedy supper, serve the meatballs on toast.

Sumac lamb meatballs with cucumber and tomato couscous

Serves 2

For the meatballs
1 tablespoon cumin seeds
10 ounces ground lamb
1 tablespoon sumac
sea salt
freshly ground black pepper
2 tablespoons light oil
2 garlic cloves, minced
14-ounce can good diced tomatoes
1 large or 2 small cinnamon sticks
handful of cilantro leaves, chopped

For the couscous
scant 1 cup couscous
4 ounces cherry tomatoes, halved
½ cucumber, quartered lengthwise
    and finely sliced
2 tablespoons extra virgin olive oil
juice of ½ unwaxed lemon

Toast the cumin seeds in a dry pan over high heat for a minute and grind with a mortar and pestle or spice grinder. Add to the lamb with the sumac and mix thoroughly with your hands. Shape into small meatballs about 1 inch in diameter. Season lightly and taste by frying off a small ball and adjusting where necessary. Fry the meatballs on all sides until brown in half the oil, in two batches if necessary. Set aside.

Sauté the garlic for 30 seconds in the remaining oil. Add the tomatoes and cinnamon and stir through. Add the meatballs and cook for 10 minutes, until cooked through.

Meanwhile, cover the couscous with boiling water in a bowl and seal with cling wrap. After 10 minutes, when the water should have been absorbed, run a fork through to fluff it up. Mix with the tomato and cucumber and dress with the olive oil and lemon. Season to taste.

Season the meatball sauce and add the cilantro, stirring through. Serve hot on top of the couscous salad.

This is a rich, addictive dish. Completely delicious, you will find yourself scooping any remaining sauce with some bread from the pan. It's reasonably quick and all the better if you use homecooked chickpeas (see page 160); it's worth the effort if you can. This has got me through many a grim winter's day.

Chorizo and chickpea stew

Serves 4

2 ounces pancetta
7 ounces cooking chorizo, in ½-inch chunks
1 garlic clove, minced
14-ounce can tomatoes
2 cups cooked chickpeas (homecooked are best, see page 160),
   or 14-ounce can chickpeas, drained and rinsed
handful of flat-leaf parsley, roughly chopped

Sauté the pancetta and chorizo in a dry sauté pan over medium heat for two minutes, until starting to crisp. Add the garlic and fry for another minute.

Tip in the tomatoes and chickpeas and cook for 20 minutes. Loosen with some water if it starts to get too thick.

Add the parsley, stir through, and serve warm with some bread.

This recipe is deceptively simple and has superb flavor. Don't be put off by the anchovies, as they cook they melt and all that is left is a gorgeously intense, savory flavor that works brilliantly with the herbs and garlic. As always, marinate the meat for as long as you can; you will reap the benefits.

Herbed lamb cutlets with anchovy

Serves 2
6 lamb cutlets
1 tablespoon minced mint leaves

For the marinade
3 tablespoons minced rosemary needles
3 tablespoons minced mint leaves
3 anchovies, minced
3 garlic cloves, minced
4 tablespoons extra virgin olive oil

The day before, combine all the ingredients for the marinade and massage into the cutlets. Cover, refrigerate, and let marinate for as long as you can and for at least four hours, or overnight is ideal.

Supper time: bring the lamb to room temperature. Fire up a grill or frying pan when you are ready to eat. There will be no need to oil the pan as there is plenty of oil on the lamb already. Fry for three to four minutes on each side for medium-rare. For larger chops, fry for a bit longer. Check their progress by cutting into one of the cutlets and taking a peek. You can also judge by checking how firm they are. Rare will feel really soft and well done very firm. You want it in the middle.

Rest for a few minutes and serve sprinkled with mint.

I have my friend Rachel to thank for the idea for this recipe. We competed in a barbecue championship and I had my usual array of spices and a very good roast chili and spice-based marinade, if I do say so myself! Rachel brought the idea of marinating some sirloin steak in lemon, bay leaves, and garlic. It was utterly delicious, really subtle, and aromatic. I had to include it here.

Sirloin is a very nice cut and is relatively reasonable, too. It deals well with marinades and is great for the barbecue, but lovely for a speedy supper at home indoors, too.

Lemon, bay, and garlic steak

Serves 2
2 x 10-ounce sirloin steaks

For the marinade
4 fresh bay leaves
finely grated zest and juice of 2 unwaxed lemons
4 garlic cloves, coarsely chopped
3 tablespoons extra virgin olive oil

The day before, combine all the ingredients for the marinade and massage into the steaks. Let marinate for at least four hours, or overnight.

Supper time: bring the steaks to room temperature. If you have a grill use that, otherwise heat a frying pan until very hot. There is no need to oil the pan as there is plenty of oil in the marinade. Cook the steak for three to four minutes on either side for medium-rare.

This recipe was born of a neighborhood hedgerow forage resulting in a lot of blackberries. I knew immediately what I wanted to do with them; combined with some rich aged balsamic vinegar, they would be perfect with some venison I had in the refrigerator. They were and it was super-quick, so it has become a favorite in the fall.

With regard to the recipe for the sauce, this—like anything you cook—requires you to taste it. The volumes of each ingredient depend on the sweetness of the blackberries, the richness of your stock, and the wine you use. It's very flexible, so feel free to adjust to your preference. Use a good balsamic if you can, as the sauce will benefit from the richness. Serve with some honest-to-goodness mashed potatoes.

Venison with blackberry and balsamic sauce

Serves 2
2 x 9-ounce wild venison steaks
sea salt
freshly ground black pepper
2 tablespoons light oil, such as canola or sunflower

For the sauce
glass of red wine (rioja or something similarly
    full-bodied works, whatever you have)
scant 1 cup blackberries
1 tablespoon balsamic vinegar
1 heaping cup meat stock (veal or light beef is best,
    but chicken works too)
1 teaspoon honey, or to taste

Pour the wine into a pan over high heat and burn off the alcohol (you will smell it in the air) for a couple of minutes. Add the blackberries, vinegar, and stock and cook over low heat for about 10 minutes, until the blackberries are cooked and mushy. Add honey to taste. Keep warm.

Ensure your venison is at room temperature. Season the steaks on each side and rub with a small bit of oil. Heat a griddle or similar until extremely hot. For a good five minutes if you can.

Fry the steaks for two to three minutes on either side for rare (which is how you should eat good wild venison), three to four for medium, five to six for well done (but please don't do that!). Rest for five minutes to allow the juices to settle, then serve on top of the warm sauce.

Flank steak is also known as skirt steak and regarded as cheap and not all that interesting. However, with a little work and time the day before, it can be really tender. It is also one of the most flavorful cuts of beef. It's still relatively cheap too, which is a bonus. That is, until everyone realizes how good it is! Flank steak is best served medium-rare as it gets very tough when cooked well.

Ask your butcher to trim it for you, removing the membranes. Miso flank steak is popping up more and more now and it's so good you can see why! It is like a tenor serenading you from your plate, absolutely irresistible.

Miso-marinated flank steak

Serves 2
2 x 10-ounce flank steaks, trimmed

For the marinade
2 tablespoons miso
2 tablespoons mirin (sweet cooking wine)
1 tablespoon soy sauce
1 red chili, deseeded and minced
1 garlic clove, minced
1-inch chunk fresh gingeroot, peeled and minced

The night before, tenderize the flank steak by hammering with a meat mallet, or bashing with a rolling pin, until half the original thickness.

Combine all the ingredients for the marinade and massage into the meat. Cover, refrigerate, and marinate overnight if possible, or for at least four hours.

Supper time: bring the steaks to room temperature. Heat a grill or frying pan until very hot. Brush excess marinade from the steak—particularly any solid bits—and fry for three minutes on each side until medium rare. Rest for three to four minutes and serve sliced.

Long Weekends

Gorgeous, simple dishes to share with friends

Weekends are a joy, for lazing, grazing, and hovering in your kitchen. The perfect time to feed friends. I like to have plenty of time to socialize with them, so I aim for low and slow cooking for the big dishes. Long roasts are ready by the time friends arrive so I can enjoy the evening with them. And don't confuse slow cooking with difficult cooking; these recipes really couldn't be easier and the results are sensational. Your friends will be very impressed.

Platters of food for sharing in the backyard, or even in your tiny London apartment in my case, make a perfect summer's evening. Most of the work is done in advance. When cooking with friends you probably want to show off a little bit. Some of the grazing recipes here are great with drinks, such as the pulled beef nachos, others as a prelude to dinner, such as the squid, others still great for snacking on, such as the chicken wings.

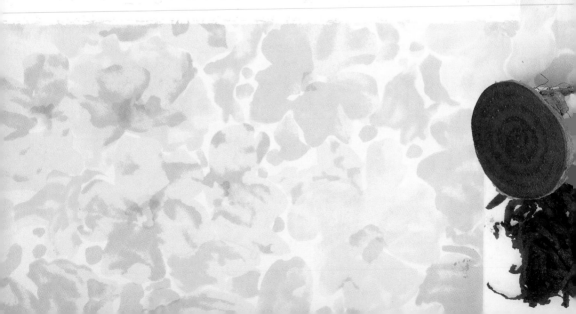

☀ PASSION ☀

Fresh cheese

Homemade cheese is a joy and so very easy. Fresh cheeses generally don't melt, but are good for cooking. One of my favorites is Indian paneer. The first time I made it many years ago, I was surprised and delighted with the flavor and texture and haven't used store-bought since. It feels rubbery and flavorless by comparison.

To make a fresh cheese, all you do is bring milk to a boil and curdle it with acid (lemon juice, white vinegar, yogurt, or buttermilk). The milk separates into curds and whey quickly. Pour it through a cheesecloth-lined strainer, drain briefly, tie in a ball, and hang it from your kitchen faucet to drain. Paneer is an everyday and very quick cheese. Ricotta (see overleaf) requires a more gentle process and you have to be mindful of its temperature. I like to lux it up a bit by adding cream to make it rich and delicious.

Make as much as you can, you might as well! These recipes are for two, but double up for four and so on. Use whole milk, or you will get a small amount of insipid cheese that isn't worth the time and effort. As with all things food, the best ingredients deliver the best results, so use the best milk and cream that you can find.

Homemade paneer

8 cups whole milk
juice of 1 unwaxed lemon (plus more in case you need it)
10-inch cheesecloth square

Bring the milk to a boil in a saucepan. Just as the milk has come to a boil, add the lemon, and stir for a minute or so as the curds and whey separate (the milk will get really clumpy). If they are not separating, add a little more lemon juice. Take from the heat—if you continue cooking the milk will get an unpleasant taste—and pour into a strainer lined with the cheesecloth. Tie the cheesecloth around the cheese with string, and hang the ball over a saucepan from your faucet to let it drain for 30 minutes or so. I am happy to use as is, however, if you want it flat, place a lid on top of it—weighted down with a bag of sugar or similar—for another 30 minutes. It's ready to use and really delicious. If you don't use it all, store it for a couple of days under water in the refrigerator.

Continued . . .

✦ PASSION ✦

Italian ricotta is very easy to make at home and is much better than most store-bought versions (unless you are buying an artisanal version). Ricotta means "twice cooked." This refers to the fact that it is a way of using up any outstanding milk solids that are lurking in whey leftover from making another cheese. Cheesemakers would cook these milk solids for a second time, adding extra milk if necessary. This home version isn't twice cooked, but observing a little sensitivity with regards to its temperature results in a very similar cheese and this is how most homestyle ricotta is made.

Homemade ricotta

8 cups whole milk
1 heaping cup heavy cream
pinch of sea salt
kitchen thermometer
juice of 1 unwaxed lemon (plus more in case you need it)
10-inch cheesecloth square

Heat the milk, cream, and salt gently to 185°F and remove from the heat. Add the lemon juice and stir gently for a minute or so until the curds and whey separate. Strain in a cheesecloth-lined colander until most of the liquid is out, then let sit for half an hour. If you want a drier cheese (for instance, if you want to use it for ricotta pancakes or for a cake), let it sit for at least an hour.

This is a lovely and really simple dip. Use it to dip crudités, or on little toasts with goat cheese, rosemary, and roasted tomatoes. Add a bowl of Chunky Guacamole (see page 47) for a feast of veggie dips.

Artichoke cream

Enough for 6 as part of a spread
9 ounces jarred or canned artichokes, drained
1 teaspoon thyme leaves
¼ cup finely grated Parmesan cheese
¼ cup extra virgin olive oil, plus more if needed
sea salt
freshly ground black pepper

Blend all the ingredients except the seasoning with a hand blender or in a food processor until it has a creamy consistency. Add more olive oil if required. Season to taste with salt and pepper.

Eggplant burned over an open flame is one of life's unexpected pleasures. The skin is charred beyond redemption but, when peeled, reveals a yielding, soft, and very smoky flesh. This dip is perfect served with toasted strips of pita or flatbread as a snack before dinner, or simply for afternoon grazing.

Smoky moutabal

Enough for 6 as part of a spread
1 large eggplant
juice of ½ unwaxed lemon
2 heaping tablespoons extra virgin olive oil, plus more to serve
2 tablespoons tahini (sesame seed paste)
sea salt
seeds of ½ pomegranate

Toast the eggplant over a gas flame, turning with tongs, until the flesh is soft and the skin is burned. Let cool, then peel off the skin under cold water.

Mash the flesh and add the lemon juice, oil, and tahini. Season with salt. Serve with the pomegranate seeds and a drizzle of oil on top.

Chorizo, white beans, and rosemary go so well together, I thought I would try an alternative way of using them and came up with this. It was an instant hit. This is a smooth and fragrant dip, an unusual twist on hummus that is a perfect partner for fried chorizo on toothpicks. It is infinitely better with homecooked beans (see page 160), but good canned beans will do if you're in a rush, or need a fix.

Cannellini bean dip with chorizo on sticks

Enough for 6 as part of a spread
For the dip
2 garlic cloves, minced
8 teaspoons extra virgin olive oil, plus more if needed
2 cups cooked cannellini beans (homemade are best, see page 160),
    or 14-ounce can cannellini beans, drained and rinsed
needles from 2 sprigs of rosemary, minced
juice of ½ unwaxed lemon
sea salt

For the chorizo
14 ounces chorizo, cut into ½-inch chunks

Sauté the garlic over medium heat in 1 tablespoon of the olive oil. Combine with all the other ingredients except the salt and blend.

Add more olive oil if needed; it will depend on the consistency of your beans. Season to taste with salt, remembering that the chorizo is salty.

Sauté the chorizo in a dry frying pan until brown and crispy on both sides. Put each piece on a toothpick (or use fondue forks, if you have them) and serve with the dip.

Potato croquettes are a fond childhood memory. When we were teenagers my sister started making them with fresh herbs and I never looked back. Mashed potatoes with herbs, bread crumbed, and deep-fried, what's not to love?

For something a little different I use mashed celery root and roll it into small ping pong-sized balls to make really good snack food for friends. Celery root is a little soggier than potato, but it does mash very well. However, my favorite way of doing these (and the quickest) is to cut the celery root into fries before bread crumbing and deep-frying, as I do here. They make perfect grazing food: different, unexpected, and delicious.

Celery root croquettes

Enough for 6–8 as part of a spread
2¼ pounds celery root
2 cups bread crumbs
1 egg, beaten
¾ cup all-purpose flour
sea salt
freshly ground black pepper
1¼ cups light oil (peanut or sunflower), to deep-fry

Cut the celery root into fries about ½ inch wide and 1¼ inches long.

Place the bread crumbs in a shallow dish, the egg in another, and the flour in a third. Season the flour well.

Coat the celery root fries first in the flour, then the egg, then the bread crumbs.

Heat the oil in a deep pan, or deep fat fryer, until a cube of bread fizzes and browns quickly when added.

Fry the celery root until the bread crumbs brown, drain on paper towels, and serve with Tarragon Mayonnaise (see opposite).

Homemade mayonnaise

Homemade mayonnaise is really luxurious and very cheap to make; it's just egg yolks, vinegar or lemon juice, mustard, and oil. It requires some concentration as the egg yolks can only absorb a few drops of oil at a time or they will split. However, it comes together a lot more quickly than you would expect and is really worth the effort. It is much easier to make with a mixer but you can do it by hand quite easily, too. Just make sure you have a large balloon whisk to make the process much more efficient.

I like to make this mayonnaise with canola oil, but sometimes make it with half sunflower and half extra virgin olive oil. Extra virgin olive oil is far too strong on its own and will dominate. Tarragon is a perfect herb for this mayonnaise but, if you can't find it, use whatever you can get. Basil and mint will make a lovely summer mayonnaise with a tomato salad; rosemary and garlic mayonnaise is delicious with lamb; horseradish mayonnaise with beef. And that's without even mentioning roast garlic mayonnaise or smoked paprika mayonnaise with fries … are you drooling yet?

Tarragon mayonnaise
with crudités

Makes about 1¼ cups
2 large egg yolks
1 teaspoon Dijon mustard
1 teaspoon lemon juice
1¼ cups canola oil, or ⅔ cup sunflower oil
and ⅔ cup extra virgin olive oil
sea salt
1 tablespoon chopped tarragon

Combine the egg yolks with the mustard and lemon juice and whisk until thickened. Add the oil, a drop at a time. After half is added, you can begin to pour it in a trickle. Season with salt and stir in the tarragon.

Serve with sliced, very fresh raw vegetables, such as peppers, carrots, and celery.

Crab is a glorious, light, and fresh ingredient. Super-healthy and wonderful with spices, it's perfect in a world of recipes. I love to make bite-size chili crab cakes for snacking on with friends. They are really easy and very tasty; the perfect solution for an afternoon or evening's entertaining.

The easiest and quickest way is to buy ready-prepared crab meat from your fishmonger. Do feel free to tackle a crab yourself though; it's very satisfying, though it takes time, and it's cheaper.

Chili crab cakes

Serves 4, or 6–8 as part of a spread
1 red chili, deseeded and minced
2 cups light oil, to deep-fry, plus 1 tablespoon
1 garlic clove, minced
1 pound 2 ounces white crab meat
4 ounces mashed potatoes (with no butter or milk added)
handful of mint leaves, minced
handful of cilantro leaves, minced
3 green onions, finely shredded
2 eggs, beaten
¾ cup all-purpose flour
sea salt
freshly ground black pepper
2 cups bread crumbs

Sauté the chili over low heat in the 1 tablespoon of oil for three to four minutes until starting to soften. Add the garlic for a minute.

Combine with the crab, mashed potatoes, herbs, green onions, and one of the eggs. Shape into small balls about the size of a ping pong ball.

Place the flour in a shallow bowl and season it well. Place the second egg in another bowl, and the bread crumbs in a third. Dip each crab cake into the seasoned flour, then the egg, then the bread crumbs.

Heat 2 inches of oil in a very large pan, or a deep fat fryer, until it reaches 350°F on an oil thermometer, or a piece of bread froths the oil when added. Fry the cakes in batches, drain on paper towels, and serve warm.

Tip: these are lovely with lime mayonnaise. Follow the recipe for Lemon Mayonnaise (see page 106), substituting lime for the lemon.

I love gravlax, but I hate dill. Now there's a conundrum! So I looked at alternative ways of making it and especially for other greenery that would love salmon and go well in a gravlax. The Japanese love fish as much as the Scandinavians so I thought about doing a Japanese version and, after having a little play, hit on shiso and sake gravlax.

You may be asking what any of that is and, if you are, I apologize! I tend to get ahead of myself. Gravlax is salmon cured with equal amounts of sugar and salt, with alcohol and other stuff like beets (very common because it is delicious). The Scandinavians often sneak some dill in there, too. It's super-easy—it just takes time—and will impress. Serve it with some good bread and you and your guests will be very happy.

Choose the best and freshest salmon you can get. Wild is best when in season but can be hard to come by, so don't worry too much about that. Good farmed organic salmon will do very well. You'll need to start the recipe three days before you need it.

Japanese gravlax

Serves 8–10
¼ cup superfine sugar
2 ounces sea salt
2 tablespoons shredded shiso leaves
2¼ pounds salmon fillet, skin on
2 tablespoons sake

Spread the sugar, salt, and shiso on the salmon and gently rub it into both sides. Sprinkle the sake on top. Place in a lidded container and store in the refrigerator for three days.

Morning and evening, baste the gravlax with the juices that collect around it. It is ready on the third day.

Wipe the marinade from the fish, slice it thinly, and serve with crackers or good bread.

I love crispy squid, especially this version. I like it a little intense so use fiery, numbing Sichuan pepper, but feel free to use just black pepper if you don't want the same effect.

Squid is cheap, sustainable, and easy to source. It also cooks super-quickly. Have your fishmonger prepare it for you if you don't think you can face it.

Salt and pepper squid

Serves 4–6 as an appetizer, or 6–8 as part of a spread
1/2 cup all-purpose flour
1/2 cup cornstarch
1 tablespoon Sichuan peppercorns, coarsely ground
1 tablespoon black peppercorns, coarsely ground
1 tablespoon sea salt
2 squid, cleaned, bodies cut into chunks, tentacles left whole
light oil, such as sunflower, to deep-fry

Combine all the ingredients except the squid and oil and mix thoroughly. Place in a shallow bowl and toss through the squid.

Heat 2 inches of oil in a very large pan, or a deep fat fryer, until it either reaches 350°F on an oil thermometer or a piece of bread froths the oil immediately when added. Fry the squid until starting to brown; no more than a couple of minutes.

Drain on paper towels and serve hot.

Chicken wings are delicious and, like a lot of delicious things, really cheap. They are perfectly moist as all the flesh is near the bone and, with so much lovely crispy skin covering it, what more do you need? I urge you to do yourself a favor and fry them. Not every day, just once in a while as a treat. They're good baked too and healthier, but fried is impossible to beat.

A note on breaking the wings. I prefer to do this as it makes them perfect finger food. Pop them with your hands by forcefully pulling at either end. Then sever the skin and flesh at the joint.

Crispy pomegranate molasses chicken wings

Serves 6–8 as a snack

For the marinade
⅔ cup pomegranate molasses
1 tablespoon cumin seeds, toasted and
   ground
1 tablespoon coriander seeds, toasted and
   ground
1 teaspoon cayenne pepper
3 garlic cloves, minced
5 tablespoons olive oil
½ teaspoon sea salt

For the chicken
2¼ pounds chicken wings, cut in half at the joint

2 whole eggs, or 3 egg whites, beaten
light oil, to deep-fry (peanut
   or sunflower)

For the seasoned flour
2 heaping cups all-purpose flour
sea salt
freshly ground black pepper
1 teaspoon cumin seeds, toasted and
   ground
½ teaspoon chili powder

Combine all the ingredients for the marinade and massage into the wings. Cover and leave in the refrigerator for at least two hours, preferably overnight. The next day, pour all the ingredients for the seasoned flour into a large plastic storage bag. Add the chicken, close the bag, and toss.

Place the eggs or egg whites in a large shallow dish. Transfer the chicken to the egg, coat thoroughly, then repeat with the flour. Heat 2 inches of oil in a very large pan, or a deep fat fryer, until it reaches 350°F on an oil thermometer or a cube of bread froths the oil immediately. Fry the chicken in batches, ensuring the pan is not crowded. Drain on paper towels and serve warm.

Tip: to make a tahini dip, chop 3 garlic cloves and crush in a mortar and pestle with a pinch of salt and 1 teaspoon of toasted cumin seeds. Add ¾ cup tahini, ¼ cup extra virgin olive oil, and 5 tablespoons of water. Add the juice of a lemon until the taste and consistency suits you. Stir in chopped cilantro and serve.

This pulled beef is fantastic, robust, full-flavored food for sharing, but you may choose to eat it on some polenta before it ever graces a plate of tortilla chips. Your choice.

It is a great recipe. Of course all of the recipes in this book are, but this has something really special, a rich, deep, lively flavor and great texture. The sauce is almost chocolatey rich, although don't let that put you off. It eats really well piled on top of polenta, but is great with the cheesy nachos, sour cream, and tomatoes here, too.

A note on brisket: it's a terrific cut and very cheap. Why it isn't on every menu, I just don't know! When cooked slowly it pulls apart gently. You can't possibly overcook it, as long as you don't have it on high heat.

Pulled beef nachos

Serves 8
For the beef
3⅓ pounds brisket, ideally on the bone
    (3 pounds off the bone)
2 tablespoons light oil
1 onion, minced
3 garlic cloves, minced
1 tablespoon cumin seeds, toasted and
    ground
1 teaspoon coriander seeds, toasted and
    ground
1 tablespoon chipotle chili flakes (or normal
    chili flakes if you can't get them)
¼ cup cider vinegar

1½ tablespoons molasses
14-ounce can tomatoes
2 bay leaves
2 cups chicken or light beef stock

For the nachos
4 ounces plain tortilla chips
⅔ cup grated mild melting cheese such
    as light cheddar
5 ounces cherry tomatoes, quartered
1 tablespoon extra virgin olive oil
⅔ cup sour cream
handful of cilantro leaves, chopped

Preheat the oven to 300°F. Brown the brisket all over in 1 tablespoon of oil over medium heat, in an ovenproof casserole or frying pan that fits the brisket. Remove from the pan and set aside.

Saute the onion in the remaining oil over medium heat for three or four minutes, stirring so it doesn't burn. Add the garlic for a minute.

Add the cumin, coriander, and chipotle and cook for two minutes. Pour in the vinegar, molasses, tomatoes, bay leaves, and stock. Stir and cook for five minutes. Return the brisket. Cover loosely with foil: you want to protect the meat, but also reduce the sauce. Place in the oven. After 1½ hours turn the brisket. Cook for another 2–2½ hours, until the brisket falls off the bone. Rest for 10 minutes, then shred the meat with two forks and mix with the sauce.

Spread the tortilla chips over a large plate and sprinkle with the cheese. Place under a hot broiler to melt the cheese. Toss the tomatoes with the olive oil. Spoon tomatoes, sour cream, and brisket over the tortilla chips and sprinkle with cilantro leaves. Serve immediately.

A traditional Spanish tapa, this translates very easily to any domestic kitchen. It's a great one to make for unexpected guests, or for quick snacks. The cider reduces into a sticky sauce, which is lovely with the bold chorizo. Cooking/fresh chorizo is best for this, but cured chorizo is fine too.

Chorizo in cider

Serves 4 as an appetizer with good toast, or 4–6 as part of a spread
1 pound 2 ounces chorizo, in ¼-inch slices
2 garlic cloves, minced
scant 1 cup cider

Sauté the chorizo in its own oil over medium heat until crispy on both sides. Add the garlic for a couple of minutes, then pour in the cider.

Reduce the cider by half and serve the chorizo on a plate with toothpicks and some good bread to mop up the juices.

These are perfect grazing food, served on bamboo skewers. Make them as big or as small as you like and serve in piles. The hot, charred, gently spiced koftes are lovely with the cooling tzatziki dip. This is a very quick dish, too, and you can make both koftes and tzatziki in advance and keep refrigerated until you need them. They will also cook well on the grill or under the broiler. You will need eight bamboo skewers (or more if you are making smaller koftes).

Turkish lamb koftes with a quick tzatziki

Makes 8 large koftes
For the koftes
1 tablespoon cumin seeds
1 tablespoon coriander seeds
2 pounds best ground lamb
1 red onion, minced
3 garlic cloves, minced
1 teaspoon chili flakes (or more if you like things hot)
handful of flat-leaf parsley, chopped

For the tzatziki
2 cups Greek yogurt
1 large cucumber, peeled, deseeded, and grated
handful of fresh mint leaves, shredded

Soak the bamboo skewers in cold water for 30 minutes, to ensure they don't burn when you put them on the grill or under the broiler.

Put the cumin and coriander seeds into a dry frying pan and place over medium heat. Stir until they smell aromatic and have turned a shade darker. Transfer to a mortar and grind to a powder with the pestle.

Combine all the ingredients for the koftes and mix well. Divide into eight portions and mold into sausages around the bamboo skewers.

Cover and refrigerate for an hour to firm up, or until you are ready to cook them.

Combine all the ingredients for the tzatziki and store covered in the refrigerator until ready to cook.

Cook the koftes on a grill or under the broiler, turning until browned on all sides. Serve with the tzatziki.

Lunch

Lunch may be light on preparation time and even portion
size, but never in flavor. Ordinarily, lunches should be
spritely. They should wake you up, not slow you down.
They need to feed and fuel you to dinner, which is a far
more serious and intense affair. These light, lively lunches
form the first half of this chapter.

However there are exceptions here which are suitable
for bitterly cold weather, especially after a brisk walk
through the snow. These heartier lunches, complete with
side dishes, make up the second half of this chapter. But
even those recipes that are heavier on meat usually contain
light and fruity elements, sharp vinegar, or fiery spices.

Most recipes are quick, a few are a little more difficult,
but I promise they are all worth it.

Homemade bread

Homemade bread is worth making just for that fantastic aroma in your home. It really isn't difficult. The ingredients are simple: flour, water, salt, and either yeast or a starter. All you do is introduce them to each other, encourage them to work together through kneading, let them bed in by allowing them to rise, then bake your lovely loaf.

Brown soda bread

Makes an 8-inch round loaf
2 tablespoons unsalted butter, diced
3 cups whole wheat flour, plus more to dust
2 cups oatmeal
1 teaspoon sea salt
1 teaspoon baking soda
1¾ cups buttermilk

Preheat the oven to 400°F.
    Add the butter to the dry ingredients and rub in with your fingers until the mixture resembles bread crumbs. Add the buttermilk and mix.
    Turn out on to a floured baking sheet and create a circle about 8 inches in diameter. Cut a deep cross in the bread.
    Bake for 30–35 minutes. The bread will be cooked when, if turned upside down and tapped, it sounds hollow.
    Cool on a wire tray, covered with a clean, dry kitchen towel.

Sourdough bread

Sourdough bread is surrounded by myth but it's really very simple. It's a way of capturing and using the wild yeasts that grow on flour and exist in the air. It results in a rich flavor that develops slowly and is worth the time and effort. Everyone has their own approach and everyone knows best. Some use rhubarb in their starter; Julia Child used grapes. At home, I simply use flour allowed to ferment with water for a week or so.
    It takes a little effort, as you have to feed the starter regularly with flour and water, but the rewards are rich. Artisan baker Tom Herbert gave me a tip for those days when you have lots of starter and no time to make bread. The answer is to make sourdough pancakes, using 9 ounces starter, ¼ cup plus 2 tablespoons of sugar, and an egg. They are the perfect combination of sweet and sour and I confess I make more of these than I do bread!

Basic sourdough starter

1½ cups whole wheat flour

Mix the flour and scant 1 cup hand-hot water thoroughly and knead for eight to 10 minutes. Place in a large jar in a warm place and leave for three days.

Feed your starter daily by throwing away half, then thoroughly stirring in scant 1 cup whole wheat flour and ⅔ cup water. When it starts bubbling it is alive (it's alive!) and is ready to use. Instead of throwing half away now, you can use it for bread or pancakes.

Basic sourdough bread

Sourdough is all about the starter; there is no need to complicate it further by using a tricky bread recipe. I prefer to keep it really simple. As you get to know your sourdough, tenderly and lovingly feeding it and watching the taste develop, you will most likely choose to expand on this recipe. It is a great starting point though and will provide you with a good, flavorful loaf. Sourdough keeps for up to a week so it will provide plentiful toast for breakfasts when it's no longer at its fresh best.

Makes 1 medium loaf
4¼ cups bread flour
2 teaspoons sea salt
5 ounces alive sourdough starter

Put your flour and salt in a large bowl, create a well in the center, and slowly add 1¼ cups water, mixing it in as you do. Then slowly add the sourdough starter. Mix with your hands, ensuring that it is well combined.

Knead thoroughly for 10–15 minutes (this depends on how much you put into it and how big you are!), until elastic and slightly shiny. Or mix in a mixer with a dough hook to get the same result. It will take some time, but frees you up to do other things.

Put in a bowl and cover with a damp kitchen towel. Store in a warm dark area—a kitchen cupboard is ideal—until doubled in size. The time this takes depends on how active your starter is, but check it after an hour. Knock it back by punching the air out. Knead again for a few minutes. Shape into a large loaf, seam at the bottom (I make it quite round), and leave for another hour. Preheat the oven to 350°F.

Cut some slashes in the top of the loaf with a knife and bake for 35–40 minutes, until a crust has formed and you get a hollow sound when you tap on the bottom.

Tip: for a good crust, spray some water into the oven after you add the bread. Also, bake on a pizza stone or tile to get a great, crispy bottom.

Blaas are a terrific bread roll from Waterford, where I am from. They are the only indigenous Irish yeast bread and are a source of county pride. We love them. A blaa is a fluffy white bread roll with a floury top, so expect to get a flour moustache as you eat them. This is my interpretation of blaas. For perfect blaas, such as those you would get in Waterford, make sure the rolls are baked very close together so when baked they join and you get soft sides when you pull them apart. I often make mine in a larger tray to get more crust, which doesn't look exactly like a blaa but still has the great flavor. Both ways work well. I sold very many of these when I had my stall at Covent Garden Real Food Market as it's the perfect vehicle for a roast meat roll and—dare I say it—a crisp sandwich. Especially with my beloved Irish cheese and onion Taytos.

Blaas

Makes 8
¼ ounce active dry yeast
2 heaping teaspoons superfine sugar
3½ cups bread flour, plus more to dust
2 teaspoons sea salt
2 teaspoons unsalted butter

Dissolve the yeast and sugar in 1 heaping cup lukewarm water. Ensure that the water is warm, not cold or hot. Leave for 10 minutes. It should get nice and frothy, indicating that the yeast is alive and well.

Sift together the flour and salt, to introduce air. Rub in the butter. Add the wet to the dry ingredients and mix until combined. Knead for about 10 minutes, until the dough is smooth and elastic. It will go from rough to a little shiny.

Place in a bowl, cover with cling wrap, and leave in a warm place for 45 minutes. Remove from the bowl and punch it down, pushing the air out the dough. Rest for 15 minutes, to give the gluten time to relax; this will make shaping easier.

Divide the dough into eight pieces. Roll each piece into a ball. Rest for five minutes more, covered.

Dust a baking dish with flour and place in the balls, side by side. Dredge with flour. Leave in a warm place for 50 minutes. Nearly there! Preheat the oven to 410°F. Dredge the blaas with flour for a final time and bake for 15–20 minutes.

Wild garlic and potato soup

Wild Garlic Pesto with Flowers (see below), glamorizes a simple bowl of potato soup.

Serves 4
2 small onions, minced
1 tablespoon light oil
2½ cups good chicken or vegetable stock
2 fresh bay leaves
1 pound potatoes, diced
1¾ cups whole milk
sea salt
freshly ground black pepper
2 tablespoons Wild Garlic Pesto with Flowers (see below)
1 tablespoon olive oil
a few wild garlic flowers

Sauté the onions in the light oil over medium-low heat until starting to soften and become translucent. Add the stock, bay leaves, and potatoes and bring to a boil. Reduce the heat to a simmer and cook until the potatoes soften (10–15 minutes). Add the milk and bring to a boil. Remove the bay leaves and blend. Season to taste.

Add half the pesto and stir through the soup. Mix the remaining pesto with the olive oil and swirl on top of each bowl, adding the deliciously oniony wild garlic flowers.

Wild garlic pesto with flowers

Makes about 1⅓ pounds
7 ounces wild garlic leaves and flowers
¾ cup grated Parmesan cheese
¾ cup walnuts
⅔ cup extra virgin olive oil, plus more to store
juice of ½ unwaxed lemon
sea salt
freshly ground black pepper

Blend everything in a blender. Season and store in the refrigerator under a film of oil.

So, you're wondering why there are so many potato soups … and why so much milk? My Irish background chooses these and they are so comforting. I love dishes that have a simple basis with something else to liven them up. Chive flowers grow in a big pompom ball; each one has many flowers. Pull them apart with your hands and you will be surprised at the delicate little flowers that form such a big ball of purple oniony intensity.

Potato soup with chive flowers

Serves 4
2 small onions, minced
1 tablespoon light oil
2½ cups good chicken or vegetable stock
2 sprigs of thyme
2 fresh bay leaves
1 pound potatoes, diced
1¾ cups whole milk
sea salt
freshly ground black pepper
handful of chives
⅓ cup extra virgin olive oil
handful of chive flowers taken from 2 big flower balls

Sauté the onions in the light oil over medium-low heat for up to 10 minutes, until starting to soften and become translucent.

Add the stock, thyme, bay leaves, and potatoes and bring to a boil. Reduce the heat to a simmer and cook for 10–15 minutes, until the potatoes are starting to soften. Add the milk and bring to a boil again. Remove the bay leaves and thyme sprigs and blend. Season to taste.

Meanwhile, blend the chives with the extra virgin olive oil to get a green oil. Serve the soup in bowls, sprinkled with chive flowers, and a drizzle of the chive oil.

Salsify is a rough, pointy-looking vegetable that you'd be forgiven for walking past in the store. However, underneath that murky rough exterior lies a creamy white, rich, and delicious root vegetable. It takes a bit of work but is worth it. Called the oyster of the vegetable world (although it really isn't fishy!), it is a natural partner for cream and wonderful in a simple gratin. When I am not using it in this way, I like to partner it with mellow, nutty roast garlic in this lovely soup. Salsify is a bit tricky, so save this for a special occasion or lovely dinner for two.

Salsify and roast garlic soup

Serves 2
1 pound 9 ounces salsify, unpeeled
squeeze of lemon juice
1 garlic bulb
extra virgin olive oil
2 large or 4 small shallots, minced
1 tablespoon olive oil
1 carrot, diced
1 potato, diced
8 cups light chicken stock
2 bay leaves
a few sprigs of thyme, plus more to serve
½ cup red lentils
sea salt
freshly ground black pepper

Scrub, scrub, scrub that salsify. Peel carefully, taking care not to strip too much of the flesh away. Chop into 1-inch sections and drop into a bowl of water with a squeeze of lemon added, so it doesn't discolor.

To roast the garlic, preheat the oven to 350°F. Slice the top from the garlic bulb, exposing the top of each clove and drizzle with extra virgin olive oil. Roast for 20 minutes and let cool, then squeeze each clove out of its papery jacket. I adore roast garlic. It should really have a chapter all of its own.

Sauté the shallots in the olive oil until translucent. Add the carrot and potato for a couple of minutes. Then add the stock, bay leaves, thyme, roast garlic, lentils, and salsify.

Bring to a boil and simmer for 20 minutes, or until the salsify is tender. Remove the thyme and bay leaf, blend in a blender, and season to taste. Serve sprinkled with thyme leaves and swirled with extra virgin olive oil. Cream would work really well, too, if you prefer.

✦ PASSION ✦

Cauliflower soup with spiced butter tortelloni

I owe the idea for this to one of my favorite London restaurants, Trinity. Spiced butter in a tortelloni melts when you boil it and, when you pierce it with your spoon, you are rewarded with a rush of gorgeous spicy butter. Homemade pasta is best and really not all that difficult if you have a mixer. It is best rolled with a pasta machine as it is hard to get thin enough with a rolling pin … I have tried!

Serves 4
For the tortelloni
2 cups pasta flour
3 egg yolks
1 tablespoon mustard seeds
1 tablespoon cumin seeds
1 teaspoon coriander seeds
1 teaspoon chili flakes
10 tablespoons butter

For the soup
2 small onions, minced
1 tablespoon light oil
1 potato, diced
2½ cups good chicken or
   vegetable stock
1¾ cups whole milk
14 ounces cauliflower florets
2 fresh bay leaves

Put the flour in a bowl and create a well in the center. Add the egg yolks and combine with a fork until a dough starts to form. Knead for 10 minutes, until the dough becomes shiny and elastic. This is easier to do in a mixer with a dough hook. Wrap in cling wrap and rest in the refrigerator for at least 30 minutes. Dry-toast the spice seeds in a frying pan for a minute or so until they start to brown and pop. Grind in a mortar and pestle with the chili and add to the butter. Combine well. Roll the pasta dough until very thin and cut into 4-inch squares. Put a teaspoon of the butter in the center and brush water around the edges. Press the edges until sealed then fold two of the corners together around your little finger and twist them to secure. Put in the refrigerator.

For the soup, sauté the onions in the oil over medium-low heat for 10 minutes, until starting to soften and become translucent. Add the potato for a minute, then the stock, milk, cauliflower, and bay leaves. Bring to a boil. Reduce the heat and simmer for 10 minutes, until the vegetables are soft. Remove the bay leaves and blend.

Boil some water and cook the tortelloni until a couple of minutes after they rise to the surface. Serve the soup in shallow bowls with three tortelloni per bowl of soup.

Pansies are delicious, pretty, and not just whimsy. As well as brightening your dish they provide vitamins A and C. They are particularly good with melon, cucumber, and lemon. I like to combine them here in a fresh and lively spring salad. This is great on its own but also good with a simple piece of white fish or chicken, or some feta to bulk it out.

Flower salad

Serves 4

12 pansies, different colors if possible
1 cucumber
½ honeydew melon
juice of ½ unwaxed lemon
3 tablespoons extra virgin olive oil
5 ounces cherry tomatoes, quartered
2 tablespoons shredded mint leaves

Wash the pansies carefully, dry them gently and very well, then trim the stalks with a pair of scissors.

Slice the cucumber lengthwise and remove the seeds by running a teaspoon down the center. Cut each piece in half again, lengthwise, then finely slice.

Peel and finely dice the melon.

In a small bowl, mix together the lemon juice and olive oil. Put the pansies, cucumber, melon, and tomatoes in a salad bowl. Pour over the dressing and toss the salad just before serving, sprinkled with the mint.

Spelt is a grain that is very easy to digest, highly nutritious, and lovely and nutty. It is used a lot in Italian cooking and increasingly so here. It is perfect for people with celiac disease—should you have one visiting or living with you—and regardless makes a gorgeous summer salad bright with tomatoes, herbs, and buffalo mozzarella. It's a great dish served on a big platter for sharing, with pita bread on the side.

Spelt salad

Serves 2
7 ounces pearled spelt
7 ounces zucchini, quartered lengthwise and minced
1 tablespoon light oil
2 garlic cloves, minced
7 ounces cherry tomatoes, quartered
9-ounce ball buffalo mozzarella, torn into small chunks
2 tablespoons shredded basil leaves
1 tablespoon shredded mint leaves
1 tablespoon good balsamic vinegar
3 tablespoons fruity extra virgin olive oil
sea salt
freshly ground black pepper

Cook the spelt in boiling water for 15–20 minutes, until tender.

Meanwhile, sauté the zucchini in the light oil for four to five minutes over medium heat until tender, then add the garlic and cook for another two minutes. Let both zucchini and spelt cool.

Gently combine all the ingredients except the balsamic vinegar, olive oil, and seasoning. Make the dressing by mixing the vinegar and oil. Dress the salad and season to taste. Serve immediately, as the dressing will make the salad soggy if left too long.

✦ PASSION ✦

Homemade wine vinegar

What to do with the ends of bottles of wine? If you ever have any, that is! Homemade wine vinegar is a bit of a revelation. We've all heard people moan that the wine in X restaurant was open too long and turned to vinegar. And they were right. Making your own vinegar can be complicated, there is bacteria you can buy and mother starters. As with most things though, there is an easier route that just takes a little more time.

Like most things that develop over time, such as sourdough bread and yogurt, a starter is required (called a "mother" for vinegar). You can develop your own starter by leaving your wine in a warm place and just letting it happen. Air is required for wine to become vinegar, so don't store it in an airtight container but cover with a cork that is slightly ajar. Add more wine (making sure it is all either white or red, not both) as you have leftover bottles. After some time, it will become vinegar. This could take anything from a few weeks to a couple of months, but once you have developed your "mother," making vinegar with it will take about a week.

To make a quick mother, you can combine your leftover wine with some cider vinegar to get it started. The flavor is better the long way though!

To make vinegar with your mother, you simply add leftover wine as you have it and it very quickly becomes an interesting new vinegar. As long as the wine was reasonably decent in the first place! Don't worry about proportions or amounts.

Homemade pizza

Homemade pizzas are a joy and so very easy. Even with the most expensive toppings they make a relatively cheap lunch. It's worth investing in a pizza stone, which should cost no more than $30. Pizzas need to be cooked at very hot temperatures and these little stone slabs, preheated in the oven before cooking, will ensure you have a perfectly crispy crust; the closest you will get to the results of a wood-fired or commercial oven.

Use fresh yeast, it gives a better flavor and texture and works more quickly. Some disagree and say you get the same results with dried yeast. It's not bad, it's true, so again don't worry too much if this is all you can get.

I consider myself to be a little bit of a pizza expert. I spent some time in Italy when younger and tried and learned lots, then came back and made many in a restaurant kitchen while at University. I used to curse making that daily enormous batch of dough, but now I look back fondly. Especially when I remember the boss going on vacation and telling the manager, "Whatever you do, don't let her make that potato pizza she's always talking about." You know what, I did. And it was really good.

For toppings, I have four favorites here (see opposite). Enjoy.

Pizza dough

Makes 8 10-inch diameter bases
¼ ounce fresh yeast, or 1 teaspoon dried yeast
2 tablespoons extra virgin olive oil, plus more to oil
2 teaspoons salt (it's best to measure here, as an unseasoned dough is an unhappy one)
4 cups bread flour, plus more to dust

It is easiest to use a mixer but I have made this by hand many times so don't worry too much if you don't have one. Measure 1¼ cups warm water. You should be able to keep your hand in it with no problems—this is important—any hotter and you will kill the yeast; you only want to wake it up. Add the water to the fresh yeast and stir thoroughly. If using dried yeast, leave it for 10–15 minutes, until it froths before proceeding. If using fresh yeast, add the oil and salt right away then add to the flour, mixing as you do.

If using a mixer, knead on medium-high speed for 10 minutes, until the dough has become elastic. You will notice it is stretchier and has taken on a sheen. You should be able to tease a ball of it with your fingers and look through it, without ripping it. By hand it's a more arduous task but very satisfying. It's the best thing to do after a bad day, I promise you! Knead vigorously on a floured surface for 10–15 minutes, until you get to the same stage.

Place it in a high-sided bowl and cover with a clean kitchen towel or cling wrap. Leave in a warm place until doubled in size; it usually takes an hour or so. Punch it down with your fists to knock the air out and let rise for about 10 minutes. It is now ready to use.

To shape, roll the dough into a long sausage, then divide into eight equal pieces. Cover with a kitchen towel or some lightly oiled cling wrap as you work with each piece.

You can roll these with a rolling pin but I prefer to mold them by hand as the rougher, more uneven results and lumps and bumps give a better texture. Just get your knuckles in and make a flat circle out of the dough about ¼ inch thick.

Spread over a couple of tablespoons of sauce, then lightly top the pizzas. Don't put on too much topping or they will be soggy and dense and go easy on the cheese. Use any cheese you like … but please, no rubbery, cheap mozzarella.

Pizza sauce

I do pizza sauce one of two ways.

In the summer, when tomatoes are in season, I roast some tomatoes gently at 300°F for an hour or so, with some thyme, fresh chili, and garlic. When they are cool, remove the skins from large tomatoes and blend in a blender.

In the winter, I use good canned tomatoes. First sauté a couple of minced garlic cloves in olive oil for 30 seconds or so, then add one can of good tomatoes and 1 tablespoon of brown sugar. Good tomatoes? Yes. Better flavor, better everything; they are worth paying extra for. A pinch of dried chili, or a small mild fresh chili, is good here too. Let the sauce cool and add a handful of chopped basil leaves.

My four favorite toppings

Bufalina. Delicious in its simplicity, just sliced buffalo mozzarella on tomato sauce, with fresh tomato slices and torn basil leaves added after it is cooked.

Artichoke cream and goat cheese. Add a few teaspoons of Artichoke Cream (see page 71) in dots around the pizza, with some goat cheese of your choice in between. Finish with some grated cheese; I like pecorino or manchego here.

Proscuitto. The quality of the ham speaks for the pizza, so use the best you can get and, if you can get it freshly sliced, it's usually cheaper and better. This pizza has tomato sauce, a little mozzarella cheese, and then a few scattered slices of ham. Finish with arugula leaves when it's cooked.

That potato pizza. I know, potato pizza, eh? But it is traditional! I first saw it in a Roman pizzeria when I was but a young 19 and determinedly re-created it myself. Slice the potatoes very thinly (preferably using a mandolin) and top the pizza with the potatoes, fontina cheese, and a little thyme or marjoram. Drizzle with extra virgin olive oil before baking so it doesn't get too dry. I love it!

I adore latkes, that delicious Jewish staple of shredded fried potato, like a mini rosti. Traditionally served with sour cream and apple sauce they are hard to beat, but I love this earthy beet interpretation. As with potato latkes, you need to squeeze the grated beet of all of its juices before adding the egg and shaping it into cakes. Horseradish is perfect with beets; you can add it to the latke as I do here, or to the sour cream if you prefer.

Beet latkes

Serves 2
5 raw beets, peeled and grated
2-inch chunk fresh horseradish root, peeled and finely grated,
    or 2 tablespoons jarred grated horseradish
1 egg, beaten
sea salt
freshly ground black pepper
2 tablespoons light oil
scant 1 cup sour cream

Squeeze all excess moisture out of the beets. It's easiest to do this with a clean kitchen towel, one whose color you don't care for. Place the grated beets inside, roll, and twist it until the towel is bright pink and the beets are as dry as you can get them.

Combine the dried beets with the horseradish, then the egg. Season, then shape into patties and shallow fry over medium heat for a couple of minutes on each side in the light oil.

Serve with the sour cream.

✦ PASSION ✦

Zucchini flowers, giant couscous

When in season, it's reasonably easy to get your hands on zucchini flowers. Ideally buy small zucchini with the female flower attached (the zucchini is actually the fruit of the female flower). Male flowers are fine too, though in this case I would suggest battering only the flower and grilling the zucchini separately.

Serves 4
For the zucchini flowers
12 small zucchini with flowers attached
(or 12 male flowers and 12 small zucchini)
$\frac{2}{3}$ cup ricotta (homemade is best, see page 70)
$\frac{1}{4}$ cup finely grated Parmesan cheese
12 mint leaves, finely shredded
scant 1 cup all-purpose flour
2 tablespoons cornstarch
light oil, for deep-frying

For the salad
scant 1 cup Israeli couscous (or normal couscous)
7 ounces baby plum or cherry tomatoes, halved
1 red onion, halved, sliced into fine rings
handful of basil leaves, torn
leaves from 2 sprigs of mint, finely shredded
2 tablespoons olive oil
juice of $\frac{1}{2}$ unwaxed lemon
sea salt
freshly ground black pepper

Remove the bitter stamens from the flowers. Combine the ricotta, Parmesan, and mint and put 1 teaspoon into each flower, folding the petals around. Cook the couscous according to the package instructions. Toss with the other salad ingredients.

Sift the flour and cornstarch and stir in scant 1 cup ice (preferably sparking) water with chopsticks or a knife, until it has the consistency of light cream. Don't worry about lumps, it's almost better to have them. Heat the oil in a pan until a piece of bread fizzes immediately. Fry the flowers and zucchini in batches; don't crowd the pan. Drain on paper towels and serve with the salad.

Eggplant is the meat of the vegetable world. It gets a bad rep as it can soak up lots of oil and is often ridiculously greasy. Cooked correctly this isn't a problem. Years ago, it was important to salt them to get rid of bitterness, but this is no longer necessary as they have been bred to exclude it. The myth still persists as an old wives' tale though.

I like to make little fritters, as squishy eggplant is perfect with a crisp crumb exterior. A nutty, sharp dressing is lovely with these. Scattered with jewel-like pomegranate seeds, it is a very pretty and delicious dish.

Crumbed eggplant fritters with pomegranate and tahini

Serves 2

For the tahini dressing
3 garlic cloves
1 teaspoon sea salt
¼ cup tahini
juice of ½ unwaxed lemon
freshly ground black pepper
1 tablespoon minced
   flat-leaf parsley

For the eggplant
2 cups bread crumbs
1 egg, beaten
¾ cup all-purpose flour
2 eggplants, in ¼-inch slices
1¼ cups light oil, such as
   peanut, to deep-fry
2 tablespoons pomegranate
   molasses, plus more to serve
seeds from 1 small pomegranate

Make the dressing. Grind the garlic cloves and salt in a mortar and pestle until it becomes a paste. Beat the tahini, garlic, and lemon, gradually adding water until you get a consistency that is like pouring cream. Season to taste and stir in the parsley. Set aside.

Place the bread crumbs in a shallow dish, the egg in another, and the flour in a third. Season the flour well. Dip the eggplant slices in the flour, then the egg, and finally the bread crumbs.

Heat the oil in a deep-sided frying pan, a wok, or deep fat fryer, until a cube of bread starts to brown immediately (or a cube of eggplant!). Add a layer of your eggplant slices and fry for two to three minutes on each side, turning halfway through.

Drain on paper towels (the eggplant will have absorbed quite a bit of oil) and serve hot with a drizzle of the dressing, another of pomegranate molasses (just a little of this), and the pomegranate seeds.

Tip: this is delicious in pita bread with some salad.

Labneh is the most simple fresh cheese. In fact it isn't a cheese at all; it is a simple strained yogurt. You need to use a thick Mediterranean-style yogurt—such as Greek yogurt—and all you do is strain it for several hours, overnight is best. You are left with a thick mass of yogurt that you can shape into little balls and marinate in flavored oils, store in jars, or use in a spritely summer dish as I do here. This is a little sweet but is still a good lunch and especially nice spread on some toast with a green salad.

Labneh with pistachio and rose

Serves 2
2 cups Greek yogurt
2 teaspoons rosewater
½ cup shelled unsalted pistachios, crushed

Make your labneh by lining a strainer with cheesecloth and suspending it over a small saucepan. Add your yogurt and let it drain overnight in the refrigerator for up to 24 hours, the longer the better.

Shape the strained yogurt into little balls and arrange in two bowls.

Add 1 teaspoon of rosewater to each and sprinkle with the crushed pistachios.

Celery root rémoulade is not very far removed from a coleslaw, but is somehow more elegant and delicate. Celery root is a favorite vegetable of mine and it's very soothing to eat. Yes, it does look a bit crazy and aggressive but don't let the knobbly root turn you off; it's delicious!

Make it ahead to allow the celery root to soften in the dressing. Homemade mayonnaise is best, but if you are stuck for time or can't be bothered, store-bought is OK, too. This makes a great lunch with good ham, pickles, and bread.

Celery root rémoulade

Serves 4–6 as part of a spread
For the mayonnaise
2 large egg yolks
1 teaspoon white wine vinegar or cider vinegar
½ teaspoon sea salt
1 teaspoon Dijon mustard
1¼ cups canola oil, or other light oil

For the celery root
1 celery root
juice of ½ unwaxed lemon
1 tablespoon Dijon mustard
handful of flat-leaf parsley, chopped

Firstly, make your mayonnaise by combining the egg yolks with the vinegar, salt, and mustard and whisking until creamy, then very slowly adding the oil as you whisk. Add the oil drop by drop initially so as not to split the egg yolks. This is easiest in a mixer, if possible.

Peel and chop the celery root into matchstick-size strips. Keep them covered with water to which the lemon juice has been added, so they don't discolor. Drain the celery root very well after it has all been chopped and add the mayonnaise, mustard, and parsley.

Stir and leave in the refrigerator for at least half an hour until the celery root has softened a little.

Tip: this is also terrific in a sandwich with leftover roast pork.

Hot-smoked salmon is easy and very satisfying to make at home. Completely different to cold-smoked fish, it is cooked through but has a gorgeous smoky flavor. If you don't like the texture of cold smoked salmon, try this. I am sure you will love it. It's also a genius use for those leftover Christmas cookie tins. You can of course buy hot-smoked salmon, but it is a lot of fun to make your own and the results are superior. I've also hot-smoked good heavy cream and made smoked butter, but that's another story …

All you have to do is drill some holes in the lid of a cookie tin, then put untreated sawdust (try your local pet store!) or some woodchips for smokers in the bottom, a wire rack on top of that (chicken wire will suffice if you don't have one that fits), and there you have it, a little hot smoker. Be warned, it does emit a lot of smoke, so use it outside if you can on a barbecue, or under a powerful exhaust fan, or by an open window at least!

Hot-smoked salmon with lemon mayonnaise

Serves 2
For the lemon mayonnaise
2 large egg yolks
1 teaspoon Dijon mustard
½ teaspoon sea salt
finely grated zest and juice of 1 unwaxed lemon
1 heaping cup light oil, such as canola, peanut, or sunflower

For the salmon
1 tablespoon light olive oil
2 x 5-ounce fillets wild or organic salmon, skin on

Make your mayonnaise first. Whisk the egg yolks with the mustard, salt, and half the lemon juice until it becomes creamy. Slowly add the oil, initially a drop at a time, then, after half has been added, in a dribble. This is to ensure that the egg yolks don't split. Add the remaining lemon juice and zest slowly at the end.

Set up the cookie tin (see recipe introduction). Place the woodchips or sawdust in the bottom with the wire rack on top. Rub the oil on the salmon and place it on the rack, skin side down. Put the lid on and place the tin over medium heat on your stovetop, or barbecue. Once you see smoke coming from the tin, it should take five to eight minutes to cook.

Remove from the tin and serve with the lemon mayonnaise and Brown Soda Bread (see page 86).

Diver-caught scallops are best for this, so ask your fishmonger for them. Dredged scallops destroy the sea bed, are full of sand and never taste as good. If possible get them in their shell with the roe attached and have your fishmonger remove them before you take both home. Samphire is a gorgeous, tender sea vegetable and is petite, salty, and sweet. It reminds me a little of asparagus; in fact it is called sea asparagus in some parts of the country. It's perfect with seafood.

Scallops with samphire and pancetta

Serves 4
4 thick slices of pancetta, cut into strips
4 handfuls of samphire, soaked in water for 30 minutes, then drained
12 scallops

Sauté the pancetta until starting to crisp and add the samphire. Stir to ensure that it is coated in the pancetta fat, then add the scallops and cook for a couple of minutes on each side. You want them to be almost sashimi raw in the center; that's when they taste best.

Eat immediately, preferably served in the scallop shells.

There are many ways to cook baby back ribs, those delicious racks of pork ribs. You can use a dry rub or a wet marinade, both allowed to mingle with the meat at least overnight; 24 hours is best. I like to use a wet marinade for this lunch recipe, a fruity, light tomato one. Most recipes use ketchup, but I use canned tomatoes instead, in the interests of keeping it light and fruity. Make as many as you can. This recipe serves four, but everyone wants more…

Baby back ribs

Serves 4
2 tablespoons cumin seeds
1 cinnamon stick, broken
14-ounce can good diced tomatoes
¼ cup honey
¼ cup red wine vinegar
3 tablespoons Worcestershire sauce
6 fresh bay leaves
2 chilies, minced
2 racks baby back ribs (there is no point
   in making just one, you will regret it!)

The day before, put the cumin seeds into a dry frying pan and place over moderate heat, stirring, until aromatic and slightly darker. Pour into a mortar and grind to a powder with the pestle (or grind in a spice or coffee grinder).

Put the cumin into a pan with all the other ingredients except the pork ribs, and heat gently until well combined. Let cool. Pour into a large plastic storage bag and add the ribs.

Seal the bag and massage the marinade well into the pork. Place in a large, shallow dish and refrigerate overnight, or for 24 hours if possible.

When ready to cook, bring the pork ribs to room temperature. Preheat the oven to 300°F. Wrap the ribs in tin foil and roast gently for 2¼ hours.

Check that the ribs are pulling away from the bone; roast for another 15 minutes if needed. Slice between the ribs with a sharp, heavy knife and serve hot.

I first had a salad like this on vacation in Granada and had to re-create it when I came home. It is so simple and makes the best of fava beans when in season. It is a little bit of a chore—OK a lot of a chore—but they are best double-podded, first removing the green pod and then the individual jackets. The sweet, gentle bean underneath is a gorgeous revelation. I like to use a Spanish jamón such as Serrano ham, but prosciutto will do too. As this recipe is Spanish I use a sherry vinegar in the dressing, which works best. Ham loves mustard, so I include some in the dressing with garlic to give it a punch.

Fava bean and ham salad

Serves 2
For the fava beans and ham
10 ounces fava beans (double-podded weight)
4½ ounces jamón serrano or prosciutto, torn into pieces
handful of flat-leaf parsley, chopped
freshly ground black pepper

For the dressing
1 tablespoon sherry vinegar
3 tablespoons extra virgin olive oil
1 garlic clove, minced
1 teaspoon Dijon mustard
pinch of sea salt

Boil the fava beans for two to three minutes, then cool in ice water or under cold running water to stop them cooking further and to preserve the gorgeous bright green color.

Whisk all the dressing ingredients together.

Combine the fava beans, ham, and parsley and toss with the dressing. Season to taste and serve.

I love quail for many reasons, one of the main being that the ratio of skin to flesh is very high, so you get a lot of fabulous crispy skin. The slightly gamey flesh takes well to marinades and cooks super quickly. Try to find quail from a source you trust and avoid intensively farmed birds. Butterflied, quail is quick to cook and easy to eat. The job is a little tricky but quick: cut out the backbone, remove the attached bones, and flatten the bird with the palm of your hand, pressing on its breastbone. It's easier to get your butcher to do it for you, but don't stress about doing it at home. I marinate it in many ways but this is one of my favorites. As always, I recommend you use fresh whole spices as you will see an enormous difference in flavor. I like to eat this with a bountiful leafy salad with a simple lemon dressing. This recipe is easy to scale up for friends.

Spiced quails with salad

Serves 2
For the quail
1 tablespoon cumin seeds
1 tablespoon sumac
1 tablespoon thyme leaves
1 garlic clove, minced
4 tablespoons extra virgin olive oil
2 butterflied quails
sea salt

For the salad
1 head lettuce
handful of tomatoes, quartered
juice of ½ unwaxed lemon
3 tablespoons extra virgin olive oil
freshly ground black pepper

Place the cumin seeds in a small dry frying pan over high heat and stir until they smell fragrant and turn a shade darker. Tip into a mortar and pestle and grind to a powder. Combine with the sumac and thyme. Add the garlic and oil and rub all over the quails. Cover and chill for at least two hours, preferably four, or even overnight.

When ready to cook, bring the quails to room temperature, season with salt, and preheat the oven to 400°F. Roast the quails for 20 minutes; they should be cooked but moist and tender.

Wash and roughly tear the lettuce and toss with the tomatoes. Dress with the lemon and olive oil and season. Serve with the quails.

I love these delicate rolls, so light and fresh with their lively herbaceous filling. If you aren't familiar with them, they look like delicious little pillows of flavor … and they are! These are also perfect for friends with celiac disease, as they are made from rice flour.

Rice paper wrappers are easier to come by now; large grocery stores and Asian food stores will stock them. They are a little tricky but with some practice come together in no time. You can always have your guests make their own for an interactive fun lunch.

If it's your first time making them, have some extra wrappers on hand as you may need to try a few before being happy with them. Larger wrappers are easier, too.

Vietnamese summer rolls

Serves 4
For the rolls
2 ounces rice vermicelli noodles
10-ounce package Vietnamese rice paper wrappers
7 ounces cooked shrimp, shelled and deveined
1 red bell pepper, deseeded and finely sliced
½ cucumber, halved, deseeded, and finely sliced
3 green onions, shredded
2 ounces bean sprouts
handful of mint leaves, chopped
handful of cilantro leaves, chopped
handful of Thai basil leaves, or normal basil leaves, chopped

For the dipping sauce
juice of 1 lime
4 tablespoons fish sauce
2 tablespoons rice vinegar
2 garlic cloves, minced
1 red chili, deseeded and minced

Cook the vermicelli according to package instructions and run under cold water to stop the cooking. Clear an area for making the rolls; you will need some elbow room! Fill a wide pan with water and soak each wrapper individually until soft, it won't take more than a minute.

In the center third place three shrimp and a little of each of the other ingredients. Not too much or it will be very difficult to roll. Fold the end facing you over the filling, then fold over the sides. Roll to the end and there you have it, a Vietnamese summer roll! Store the rolls under cling wrap in the refrigerator so that they don't dry out.

Mix the ingredients for the dipping sauce and serve it with the rolls.

These may be fried but they are really light and zesty with a bit of a kick. A gentler take on a spring roll (although they work really well with spring roll wrappers too), these summer rolls can be eaten fresh, but I can't resist frying them. Ground pork shoulder is best for this; it has the appropriate level of fat content and also has great flavor.

Lemongrass is great with pork and makes me think of sunshine and vacations. The stalks may look confusing; what to do with that? But when you remove the outer layers and mince the stems, you have a fantastic, full-flavored and aromatic ingredient. As such it is important not to use too much.

When you fry the rolls, the meat crumbles, so when you bite in you find little pork crumbles fugitive among the noodles. I think I might have to run off and make some more now.

Fried aromatic pork summer rolls

Makes about 20 rolls
2 lemongrass stalks, trimmed
  and minced
2 garlic cloves, minced
1 red chili, deseeded and minced
1-inch chunk fresh gingerroot, minced
light oil, for deep-frying
14 ounces ground pork shoulder,
  or best ground pork

2 ounces rice vermicelli noodles
handful of mint leaves, chopped
handful of cilantro leaves, chopped
3 green onions, shredded
2 ounces bean sprouts
1 carrot, grated
10-ounce package Vietnamese rice
  paper wrappers (or spring roll
  wrappers)

Fry the lemongrass, garlic, chili, and ginger in 1 teaspoon of the oil for a couple of minutes. Add the pork and stir for about five minutes, until brown and cooked through. Meanwhile, cook the noodles according to the package instructions, drain, then cool under running water.

Arrange the ingredients in bowls or on a plate: pork, herbs, green onions, bean sprouts, carrot, and cooked noodles.

Fill a wide pan with water and soak each wrapper individually until soft; it won't take more than a minute. Take care not to tear them; they will be delicate when soft. (Skip this step if using spring roll wrappers.)

Put a wrapper on a plate and make a 2 x 1-inch rectangle of a little of all of the ingredients, placing it about 1 inch from the end closest to you. Fold the end over it, then fold over the sides, then roll to the end. Take care not to tear them, as they will burst when you fry if they have any holes. Fry in a shallow pan with about ½ inch of hot oil, turning to ensure all sides are crispy, or deep-fry until crispy. Drain and serve with the dipping sauce opposite.

I love lentils and think they are much underrated, I often reach for this shepherd's pie recipe over a meaty version as a result. It's a great sharing dish for veggie friends, served in the middle of a table with a big spoon for everyone to help themselves. It's also great for January, when wallets and constitutions are suffering.

Lentil shepherd's pie

Serves 6

For the lentils
1 carrot, quartered and minced
2 celery stalks, finely sliced
1 tablespoon light oil
2 garlic cloves, minced
3⅓ cups vegetable stock
sprig of thyme
1 bay leaf (optional, but gives lovely fragrance)
1¼ cups green or French green lentils
½ cup red lentils
sea salt
freshly ground black pepper

For the mashed potatoes
1¾ pounds good mashing potatoes, peeled
2 tablespoons cream or milk (depending on how indulgent you
    are feeling!)
1 teaspoon grainy mustard
¼ cup cheese (soft goat cheese or grated cheddar both work well)
handful of flat-leaf parsley, chopped

Preheat the oven to 350°F.

Sauté the carrot and celery in the oil over low heat for 10 minutes, until starting to soften. Add the garlic for the final minute.

Add the stock, thyme, bay leaf, if using, and lentils and bring to a boil. Reduce the heat and simmer for about 20 minutes, until the lentils are tender. Season to taste and set aside.

Boil the potatoes until soft (a knife will go through easily but they won't be too mushy). Mash with the cream or milk. Add the mustard, cheese, and parsley and stir through.

Put the lentils in a deep baking dish (about 8 x 8 inches). Spread the mashed potatoes on top and decorate with the tines of a fork so that you get ridges which will crisp nicely as it roasts.

Roast for 15 minutes and serve hot.

I love this dish, especially when made with lovely light and creamy Homemade Paneer (see page 68). It's perfect for healthy veggie days and hot summer lunches. The main ingredients are super-simple, the spices bring out the best in everything. Frozen peas are fine for this but if you can get fresh in-season peas in the pod, even better. Serve with pita bread, naan bread, or rice.

Mutter paneer

Serves 2

For the mutter paneer
1 tablespoon coriander seeds
1 teaspoon cumin seeds
10 peppercorns
2 tablespoons light oil
2 shallots, minced
1-inch chunk fresh gingerroot, minced
½ teaspoon turmeric
1 teaspoon garam masala
1 red chili, deseeded and minced
   (keep the seeds in if you're a heat freak)
1 large garlic clove, minced
14-ounce can diced tomatoes

1 tablespoon superfine sugar
9 ounces paneer, diced (homemade
   is best, see page 68)
1¾ cups frozen peas
sea salt
juice of 1 unwaxed lemon
handful of cilantro leaves, chopped

For the salad
8 cherry tomatoes, quartered
handful of cilantro leaves, chopped
a little red onion, finely sliced
a little lemon juice (should be enough
   left from the lemon above)

Dry-fry the coriander and cumin seeds until fragrant, then grind with the peppercorns in a mortar and pestle.

Heat 1 tablespoon of the oil and add the shallots over gentle heat. Cook until starting to soften. Add the ginger and cook for a minute before adding the freshly ground spices, turmeric, garam masala, and chili. Stir thoroughly and cook for another few minutes. Stir in the garlic and cook for a minute more. Add the tomatoes and sugar and cook over low heat for 10 minutes while you work on the paneer.

Fry the paneer in a separate pan in the remaining oil until browning all over. When the paneer is ready, add the peas and ⅓ cup water to the sauce, increase the heat, and bring to a boil. Reduce the heat to low and add the paneer.

Cook for another five minutes. Meanwhile, mix all the ingredients for the salad with a little lemon juice, to taste. Season the mutter paneer with salt and add lemon juice and cilantro to taste. Serve immediately.

I have a soft spot for buttermilk. I saw quarts of it gracing store refrigerators as I grew up in Ireland, where it is used in everyday cooking for soda bread. If you can't source buttermilk, you can fake it by acidulating 2¾ cups whole milk with ⅓ cup plain unsweetened yogurt.

Buttermilk is a perfect marinade, tenderizing meat and giving a lovely sourness, similar to yogurt. This recipe makes decadent and delicious chicken nuggets that are impossible to resist. I like to use chicken thigh meat, as it is moist and more flavorful than breast.

If you don't want to fry you can roast these on an oiled tray for 25–30 minutes at 350°F. Turn halfway through cooking to ensure that both sides crisp.

But do fry these if you can; it's important to have an occasional treat!

Buttermilk fried chicken

Serves 6–8 as a snack
3 cups buttermilk
2 garlic cloves, coarsely chopped
needles from 2 sprigs of rosemary, minced
1⅓ pounds chicken thigh meat, cut into nugget-size portions
¾ cup all-purpose flour
sea salt
freshly ground black pepper
2 eggs, beaten
2 cups bread crumbs
light oil, to deep-fry (sunflower or peanut are ideal)

Mix the buttermilk, garlic, and rosemary together in a shallow dish. Add the chicken; cover, and refrigerate overnight if you can, or for at least four hours. The chicken will benefit immensely from it. Take the chicken from the marinade and let the excess drain off on paper towels.

Place the flour in a shallow bowl and season it well. Place the eggs in another bowl and the bread crumbs in a third. Coat the chicken pieces in the seasoned flour, then in the egg, then the bread crumbs. If the coating isn't sticking, repeat the egg and bread crumb part again.

Heat 2 inches of oil in a very large pan, or a deep fat fryer, until it either reaches 350°F on an oil thermometer, or a piece of bread froths the oil immediately when added. Fry the chicken in batches; don't crowd the pan. Drain on paper towels and serve with toothpicks.

This is a lively, bold salad full of energy and health. It's a slaw really. Raw veggies are packed with goodness and—don't tell anyone I told you—beets are detoxifying and good for your liver, so roll this one out for hangovers. The ginger in the dressing is also superb for a tummy ache. Try this salad with Vietnamese Summer Rolls (see page 112).

Carrot and beet salad with sesame and orange dressing

Serves 4
For the salad
2 large raw beets, peeled and grated
3 carrots, grated
3 green onions, shredded
1 tablespoon sesame seeds

For the dressing
3 tablespoons freshly squeezed orange juice
2 tablespoons peanut oil, or other flavorless oil
1-inch chunk fresh gingerroot, minced or grated
sea salt
freshly ground black pepper

Make the dressing by whisking together all the ingredients and seasoning with salt and pepper.

Toss the beets, carrot, and green onions just before serving (the beets will turn everything pink if you leave it too long), combine with the dressing, and serve with the sesame seeds sprinkled on top.

Tomato in béarnaise sounds like it wouldn't work, but the acidity and sweetness is really delicious and it makes a gorgeous dip here. Purple sprouting broccoli is very reasonably priced and, I think, as impressive and flavor-packed as asparagus. It makes great sharing food. People won't have tried this before either, so you will be on to an impressive winner. Try it with Beef, Beet, and Horseradish Burgers (see page 121).

Homemade béarnaise is a little tricky but the results are worth it. Aniseedy tarragon adds a lovely edge and roasted tomato a fruity layer. This sauce is also great with steak.

Purple sprouting broccoli with tomato and tarragon béarnaise

Serves 4–6
10 ounces purple sprouting broccoli

For the béarnaise
1 large tomato, peeled
1 banana shallot, or 3 normal shallots, minced
8 tablespoons (1 stick) unsalted butter
¼ cup white wine vinegar
¼ cup dry white wine
3 egg yolks
sprig of tarragon, minced
sea salt
freshly ground black pepper

Preheat the oven to 300°F. Roast the tomato for 30 minutes, until soft. Deseed and mince.

Fry the shallots in a little of the butter over medium heat until soft and transparent, not brown, about five minutes. Add the vinegar and wine and reduce over medium-high heat until it has halved in volume.

Melt the butter and set aside. You will need to use the béarnaise as soon as it's ready so, as the butter is melting, steam or roast your purple sprouting broccoli for five minutes, until tender but still firm.

Take the shallot mixture from the heat and slowly whisk in the egg yolks, taking care that they don't split. Slowly add the butter, whisking as you go. Finish with the tarragon and tomato and season to taste.

Sprinkle the broccoli with sea salt and serve with the béarnaise either drizzled over or as a dip on the side.

Earthy beets and pungent, spicy horseradish work brilliantly with the ground steak in these burgers. I like the beets raw; finely grated they blend with the meat quite well. Cooked will work too. Be warned, this is messy but oh, so satisfying. Your hands will turn bright pink as you prepare the burgers. They are best made and cooked immediately; if you let them sit in the moisture from the beets, it will make the burgers a little soggy. There is no need to add anything like bread crumbs or egg as some burger recipes do; they only make steak go further if you are trying to spare it; and you sacrifice flavor and texture when you do. Try not to overcook them. If you have good ground steak, you should eat these burgers medium rare, when they will have the best flavor and texture. Salt just before you cook too, as salting earlier will result in a loss of moisture and a tough burger. Nobody wants that!

Beef, beet, and horseradish burgers

Makes 8
2¼ pounds best ground beef (chuck steak works well for this)
2 raw beets, peeled and finely grated
2-inch chunk fresh horseradish root, finely grated
sea salt

Combine all the ingredients except the salt in a bowl and mix thoroughly with your hands. Divide the mixture into eight equal balls, each about 4½ ounces in weight. Shape each into a circle and squash down until they are burger shaped.

Cook on a hot griddle or frying pan for three to four minutes on either side, salting only after you turn them over, until still bouncy and moist. Burgers are best served medium rare and, if you have invested in good beef, you will really appreciate it.

✦ PASSION ✦

Homemade tomato ketchup

Made with good canned tomatoes, this is a pleasure and is actually very quick. I really don't enjoy the processed, oversweet flavors of most commercially available tomato ketchups and so avoid them. I like my ketchup to be tangy and have some heat, and I like it to have some texture too. I find it's easiest, tastiest, and quite cheap to make my own. Ideally we would use in-season fresh tomatoes at their best but, in this part of the world, the season is short and the fruits often expensive. However, if you are making this recipe in the summer, do feel free to substitute the canned tomatoes with 2¼ pounds peeled and deseeded fresh lovely tomatoes.

Makes about 4 cups
1 red onion, minced
1 tablespoon light oil
2 garlic cloves, minced
1 red chili, deseeded and minced
2 x 14-ounce cans good sweet canned tomatoes, such as San Marzano or similar
¼ cup brown sugar
⅓ cup cider vinegar
1 small cinnamon stick
1 bay leaf
sea salt
freshly ground black pepper

Sauté the onion in the oil over medium-low heat for about five minutes, until starting to soften. Add the garlic and chili and cook for a minute. Add the tomatoes, sugar, vinegar, cinnamon, and bay leaf and bring to a boil. Reduce the heat and cook over low heat for 45 minutes or so. Remove the bay leaf and cinnamon stick.
Season to taste.

I like my ketchup chunky like this but, if you like it smoother, blend and pass through a strainer. This ketchup will keep for a week in the refrigerator, preferably in an airtight jar.

Roasted slowly on the bone, lamb shanks are rich and tender and retain a lot of moisture. I like to marinate shanks in a dry spice rub, here a North African ras el hanout with aromatic dried rose. You can dry your own roses for this (if you haven't put pesticides on them!), or buy them online. It's worth the effort for the lovely quality they impart.

Ras el hanout lamb shanks with couscous

Serves 4

For the ras el hanout
1 tablespoon cumin seeds
1 tablespoon coriander seeds
1 tablespoon black peppercorns
seeds from 8 cardamom pods
2 large cinnamon sticks, broken up
1 tablespoon turmeric
10 dried rose buds or ¾ ounce dried rose petals
1 tablespoon sea salt

For the lamb and couscous
4 lamb shanks
4 tablespoons light oil
2 carrots, halved lengthwise and finely sliced
2 celery stalks, finely sliced
1 onion, minced
2 garlic cloves, minced
14-ounce can good tomatoes
2 cups lamb or chicken stock
1 tablespoon superfine sugar
1¾ cups couscous

Make your ras el hanout by first toasting the whole spices in a dry pan over medium-high heat. Add the turmeric and rose buds and grind in a mortar and pestle or spice grinder with the salt.

Rub the ras el hanout into the lamb shanks, cover, and leave for at least two hours in the refrigerator. Take them out and bring them to room temperature. Preheat the oven to 325°F.

Heat the oil in a large ovenproof pan that can hold the shanks—about a three-quart pot—and brown the lamb shanks on all sides. Remove from the pan and set aside. Fry the carrots, celery, and onion over medium-low heat for eight to 10 minutes, until softened. Add the garlic for one minute. Add the tomatoes, stock, sugar, and lamb. Cover and put in the oven for 2½ hours, until the meat pulls away from the bone.

Let rest for 15 minutes. Meanwhile, tip the couscous into a bowl and cover with boiling water. Seal with cling wrap and, after 10 minutes, fluff it up with a fork. Season and serve with the lamb shanks.

Much larger than pork ribs, beef ribs are also packed with flavor as is anything next to the bone. They are great for barbecues but work really well cooked slowly in the oven. Lots of spices will work here, but I like to use a strong paprika and chili base to give the illusion of smokiness in oven-baked ribs. Molasses, a deeply savory, sweet, and sticky sugar syrup which is a by-product of the sugar production process, is super-intense and licoricelike on its own but, with red wine vinegar to balance, is terrific with beef.

Ask your butcher for the ribs; they will usually be only too delighted to provide them, if they are willing to part with them! Ask your butcher to prepare them and cut them into short ribs. This is another low, slow cook (what else are weekends for?), but you will be rewarded with sweet, smoky, sticky ribs, perfect with buttery mashed potatoes.

Spiced slow-roast short ribs

Serves 4
3⅓ pounds beef short ribs, trimmed
3 tablespoons light oil

For the marinade
3 tablespoons molasses, or ¼ cup soft dark brown sugar (the sticky one)
scant ⅓ cup red wine vinegar
4 tablespoons soy sauce
1 tablespoon Worcestershire sauce
4 garlic cloves, chopped
2 tablespoons cumin seeds, roasted and ground
2 tablespoons mild Spanish paprika
4 tablespoons tomato ketchup (homemade is best, see page 122)

Combine all the ingredients for the marinade and massage it into the ribs in a pan large enough to hold them. Cover and refrigerate for at least two hours, taking them out half an hour before cooking.

Preheat the oven to 300°F. Take the ribs out of the marinade and let the excess drip off. Reserve the marinade. Fry the ribs in half the oil in batches, until brown on all sides. Place in a roasting tray oiled with the remaining oil, cover with foil, and put in the oven.

After 1½ hours, turn the ribs and brush with the marinade. Cover again and continue to roast for another 1½ hours. They should be meltingly tender. Remove from the oven and rest for 20 minutes.

Meanwhile, make a sauce by pushing the remaining marinade through a strainer and bringing to a boil, reducing to half its volume over medium heat. Serve with the short ribs.

Potato dauphinois is a classic creamy dish that I updated slightly and adapted to my taste one day while exploring the contents of my pantry. It worked really well, so since then I have made it again and again.

I find sweet potatoes too sweet on their own, so combining them with normal potatoes works perfectly. There isn't as much cream in this dish as you would expect either. This is lovely with a salad or with some simple broiled meat on the side.

Potato and sweet potato dauphinois

Serves 4
2 garlic cloves, minced
1 teaspoon light oil
5 tablespoons heavy cream
needles from 1 sprig of rosemary, minced
1 bay leaf
9 ounces large waxy potatoes, peeled
9 ounces sweet potatoes, peeled

Preheat the oven to 350°F. Sauté the garlic in the oil over medium heat for 30 seconds, then add the cream, rosemary, and bay leaf. Bring to a simmer and turn off the heat. Set aside to allow the herbs and garlic to infuse.

Using a mandolin, finely slice the potatoes into circles. If you don't have a mandolin use a knife, but do slice as finely as possible.

Take the bay leaf out of the cream and pour the cream over the potatoes. Mix thoroughly with your hands, ensuring that all the slices are coated with cream.

Layer in an ovenproof dish and roast for about 40 minutes; the potatoes will be tender and browning on top. Check for tenderness by piercing the dauphinois with a knife; it should meet no resistance at all until it gets to the bottom of the dish.

Serve warm.

Roast bone marrow with a Parmesan crust

Any roast bone marrow dish from me will have to give a nod to Fergus Henderson of St. John, the only reason I ever tried it in the first place. Roast bone marrow is a very rich and intensely savory, umami-packed dish. It is beautiful simply roasted, scooped out of the bone, and spread on toast. I also use it as a secret ingredient in beef-based sauces: minced raw bone marrow gives my Gutsy Ragu with Gremolata an extra savory depth and richness (see page 140).

One bone per person is plenty and it makes a perfect lunch, or even an appetizer (though make sure your entree is lighter). It's so dramatic looking that some of your friends may be taken aback; get them to try it and they will change their minds.

Serves 8
handful of flat-leaf parsley, minced
¾ cup dried bread crumbs
¼ cup finely grated Parmesan
sea salt
8 bone marrow shafts, halved vertically or horizontally
(whatever your butcher can provide), with extra meat on
the bone removed (your butcher can do this)

Preheat the oven to 350°F. Combine the parsley, bread crumbs, and Parmesan and season with a little salt.

Place the bones in a roasting tray with the largest bone marrow surface facing up. Cover the exposed bone marrow with the bread crumb mixture. Roast for 15–20 minutes, until the marrow is starting to soften and is buttery in texture.

Serve spread on good sourdough toast with some of that lovely crust mixed in.

Lamb breast is a very cheap cut; it's basically the belly of the lamb or ribs. Many butchers throw it away as it's not worth the effort to get the meat off the bones for the grinder and, as it is quite fatty, it has fallen out of favor in our fat-obsessed times. It is silliness really; fat—in moderation—is not bad for you. And it is where the flavor lies.

Lamb breast with persillade crust

Serves 6
2 tablespoons light oil
2 lamb breasts, trimmed, with
   a layer of fat remaining on top
2 handfuls flat-leaf parsley, chopped
6 garlic cloves, minced
2 cups bread crumbs
1 tablespoon sea salt

Preheat the oven to 400°F.
   Oil two baking trays that will fit the lamb breasts and place one breast in each tray, fat side up.
   Combine the parsley, garlic, bread crumbs, and salt and spread liberally over the top.
   Roast for 20 minutes. Remove from the oven and cover with foil. Reduce the oven temperature to 350°F. Roast for another 1½ hours.
   Let rest for 10 minutes before serving. The lamb is quite rich so this goes really well with some salad.

Slow-cooked pork cheeks in cider

Pork cheeks are super-cheap and delicious. My mother used to tell us—to frighten us into eating our stew—that she and her sisters fought over the cheeks on the pig's head they had for dinner, as it is the best bit. It really is.

Full-flavored and rich, cheeks benefit from a long, slow cook and are lovely braised, darker than other cuts. Like anything that takes time, it is worth making extra. Leftovers are especially good as a pie filling; think cold winter evenings and solace.

Pig's cheeks are becoming increasingly easy to source; you can ask your butcher to reserve some for you.

Serves 4–6
5 shallots or 2 onions, minced
2 tablespoons light oil
3 garlic cloves, minced
2¼ pounds pork cheeks, trimmed by your butcher
2 cups hard cider
1 tablespoon Dijon mustard
3 cups chicken or pork stock
2 bay leaves
handful of flat-leaf parsley, chopped

Sauté the onions in half the oil over medium heat for about five minutes, until they start to soften without going brown. Add the garlic and sauté for a minute or so.

In a separate pan, brown the pork cheeks in the remaining oil in batches, taking care not to crowd the pan, otherwise they will stew.

Add the pork to the garlic and onion and deglaze the pork pan with a little of the cider, to mop up all of those lovely porky bits. Add to the pork with the rest of the cider, bring to a boil, and reduce the cider by about one-third. Add the mustard, stock, and bay leaves; reduce the heat; cover and cook gently over low heat on the stove for 2½ hours, stirring occasionally. (Alternatively, cook, covered, in an oven preheated to 300°F for the same time.)

Check that the pork is fork-tender and pulls away at the slightest touch; that's when it is done. Remove from the heat and stir in the parsley. Serve hot.

Eight Great Big Dinners...

...and what to do with the leftovers

I love cooking for a crowd and find big joints of meat dramatic, delicious, and a joy to tuck into. Far more often than that though, I cook a joint for only a small group of friends—sometimes just for me—which presents me with the joy of leftovers. Far from being an annoyance, most things taste better the next day and are great to cook with and to eat. Some good pastry transforms the humble leftover into a wonderful pie. Dumpling wrappers with leftover roast meat make superb dumplings that can be dropped in a soup made from the leftover bones.

And it's not only meat that keeps on giving. I present you with the humble potato: leftovers sliced and fried become delicious, crispy sautéed potatoes; mashed and combined with fish and herbs, a gorgeous fish cake. These days, I deliberately cook extra to save time and make life easier.

I often roast large pumpkins and squash; in fact once I roasted a specimen that was two feet high! Although that was an unusual gift from a local allotment, delivered in segments in a cement bag, I do roast large squashes in segments so I can use the pumpkin over the following days or freeze to use later. It makes life more efficient and sweeter.

One of my regular weekend chores is batch cooking lots of beans. Why? They taste better than canned, they're super-cheap and, after I freeze them in 2-cup amounts, they're available for stews, soups, bean mashes, or anything for weeks to follow.

This chapter includes some of my very favorite ways of BIG cooking. I encourage you to adopt the habit. Far from making your life more difficult, it will simplify it, making eating well far cheaper and your food tastier.

When I had my stall at Covent Garden I wanted the tastiest, most luscious lamb for my homemade bread roll sandwiches, but I needed to sleep to survive my crazy 17-hour days. So I developed this overnight lamb recipe, which greeted me with wafts of deliciousness as I made my way down the stairs ready to start a day's work. You can, of course, cook it in the morning for dinner that night.

Cinnamon is wonderful with lamb, reminiscent of fall evenings or summer barbecues. Grind your own cinnamon, and you'll be rewarded tenfold in flavor.

This will feed many more in sandwiches or picnic wraps. I serve it with my Smoky Eggplant Relish (see page 134), but anything tomato-based will work really well.

When thinking leftovers, remember lamb loves mint, coriander, sumac, cumin, eggplant, and tomato, so feel free to play around with these flavors. The leftover lamb is tender and rich and works well in many different places. My favorites follow this recipe.

Overnight shoulder of lamb

Serves 4–6

2 tablespoons cumin seeds
4 cinnamon sticks, or 1½ tablespoons ground cinnamon
2 red chilies, deseeded and minced
4 garlic cloves, minced
2-inch chunk fresh gingerroot, minced
sea salt
a little oil, sunflower or olive will do fine
1 x 5½-pound whole shoulder of lamb
6 tomatoes, halved

Toast the cumin seeds over high heat in a dry pan. Grind with a mortar and pestle (or spice or coffee grinder) with the cinnamon to a powder. Add the chili, garlic, and ginger and grind some more. Add salt to taste and enough oil to make a paste, then rub it all over the lamb. Cover and marinate in the refrigerator for as long as you can; at least two hours.

When you're ready to cook, bring the lamb to room temperature. Preheat the oven to 425°F. Place the lamb in a deep roasting tray and roast for 20 minutes. Remove from the oven and reduce the temperature to 212°F. Add the tomatoes to the roasting pan, cover with foil, and place in the oven for 8¾ hours, while you sleep or get on with your day!

The lamb will be creamily tender with lovely seasoned skin. Rest for 30 minutes before eating with the sticky, almost datelike tomatoes.

Tip: while your oven is on for a long time at a low temperature, it's the perfect opportunity to slow-roast vegetables if you have room.

Pairing lamb and eggplant again, I know, but they are so good together. This is like a Middle Eastern caponata, the Italian eggplant stew, with some lamb in!

Lamb and eggplant stew

Serves 4
1 tablespoon cumin seeds
1 red onion, minced
1 small eggplant, chopped
2 tablespoons olive oil
2 garlic cloves, minced
1 red chili, deseeded and minced
1 pound 2 ounces leftover lamb shoulder, in large chunks
14-ounce can good diced tomatoes
1 tablespoon sumac
sea salt
freshly ground black pepper
handful of cilantro leaves, chopped

Toast the cumin seeds over high heat in a dry pan. Grind with a mortar and pestle (or spice or coffee grinder) to a powder.

Sauté the onion and eggplant in the oil over medium-low heat until starting to soften. Add the cumin, garlic, and chili.

Add the lamb, tomatoes, and sumac. Bring to just before a boil and let simmer gently for 20 minutes.

Season to taste and finish with the cilantro leaves. Serve with toasted bread, couscous, or rice.

This is a gorgeous, rustic, and flavorful use of leftover lamb shoulder. It also costs just cents and is ridiculously simple. Serve with the smoky eggplant relish.

Lamb and potato cakes

Serves 4 for a snack, or 2 for supper
For the smoky eggplant relish
2 eggplants
4 roast tomatoes (roasted with the lamb
    shoulder, if you have any left)
2 tablespoons tahini
1 tablespoon pomegranate molasses
1 tablespoon sumac
1 tablespoon cumin, toasted and ground
1 red chili, deseeded and chopped
handful of cilantro leaves, chopped

For the potato cakes
1 pound 2 ounces potatoes, peeled
sea salt
2 tablespoons unsalted butter
12 ounces leftover lamb shoulder, shredded
3 green onions, minced
⅓ cup all-purpose flour, plus more to dust
handful of flat-leaf parsley, chopped
freshly ground black pepper
2 tablespoons light oil

To make the relish, burn the eggplants all around over a gas flame until black and squishy. Let cool and peel the skin off. Don't worry if you can't get it all off. Mash the flesh. Combine with the other ingredients except the cilantro and roughly blend, leaving in some chunks.

Put the potatoes in a large pan of salted water, bring to a boil, and simmer for 15 minutes, or until tender to the point of a knife. Drain well and mash. Melt the butter in a small saucepan. In a large bowl, combine the lamb, mashed potatoes, butter, green onions, flour, parsley, and seasoning. Flour your hands, and collect a handful of the mixture. Shape into a ball and flatten. Repeat until all the mixture has been used.

Heat the oil in a large frying pan over medium heat. When hot, add the potato cakes, making sure not to crowd the pan (you may have to fry in batches). Cook for three to four minutes on either side until browned.

Stir the cilantro through the relish and serve with the potato cakes.

Samosas are terrific comfort food. Samosa wrappers are available from Asian food stores and most grocery stores, but it's easier to find phyllo pastry, which is what I use here. These are very quick to make and, once you have got the hang of rolling them into triangular packages, they take just seconds to assemble. Once rolled they also freeze very well, each wrapped individually in wax paper. That's just in case you can't face eating lamb five days running…

Spiced lamb samosas

Serves 4
1 tablespoon cumin seeds
½ onion, minced
1 tablespoon light oil
1 pound 2 ounces leftover lamb shoulder, chopped
1⅓ cups frozen peas, defrosted
9 ounces phyllo pastry
4 tablespoons unsalted butter, melted, or ⅔ cup olive oil
light oil, to deep-fry (optional)

Toast the cumin seeds over high heat in a dry pan. Grind with a mortar and pestle (or spice or coffee grinder) to a powder.

Fry the onion in the oil with the cumin until soft. Transfer to a bowl and add the lamb and peas. Combine well, using your hands.

Cut the phyllo pastry into rectangles, each about 8 x 4 inches. Lay them out and brush liberally with butter or oil. Put 1 tablespoon of the meat filling about 2 inches in from one end of the pastry.

Fold the pastry edge over the filling to form a triangle, then roll to the end, keeping the triangle shape. Repeat to use up the lamb.

Samosas are best deep-fried. Heat 2 inches of oil, if using, in a very large pan, or a deep fat fryer, until it reaches 350°F on an oil thermometer, or a piece of bread froths the oil immediately when added. Fry samosas in batches until golden, drain on paper towels, and serve warm.

These are good cooked in the oven too, if you prefer; bake in a preheated oven at 350°F for about 25 minutes.

I love these and used to sell them at my market stall. Use store-bought pastry (puff or piecrust) if you wish, but I love to use homemade butter-rich piecrust. I like to make big chunky rolls that would satisfy for a whole meal. They make terrific picnic lunches.

Lamb and smoky eggplant rolls

Makes 4 chunky sausage rolls
For the piecrust pastry
1 heaping cup all-purpose flour, plus more to dust
sea salt
6 tablespoons unsalted butter, chilled and diced
1 egg, beaten

For the filling
1 large eggplant
2 garlic cloves, minced
1 tablespoon olive oil
1 pound 2 ounces leftover lamb shoulder, chopped
1 heaping tablespoon sumac
handful of cilantro leaves, chopped
freshly ground black pepper
1 egg, beaten

First make the pastry: sift the flour with a little salt and add the butter. Rub quickly with your fingers until it looks like bread crumbs. Add the egg and bring together with a knife (to keep it cool). Add a little water if needed. Shape into a ball, wrap in cling wrap, and chill for an hour.

Blacken the eggplant over a gas flame, rotating until it looks like there is no hope ... that's when it's perfect! Let cool. Preheat the oven to 400°F. Sauté the garlic in the oil for a minute. Place the lamb and sumac in a bowl and add the garlic. Peel and chop the eggplant (don't worry about little bits of skin that stubbornly remain). Add to the lamb with the cilantro. Season to taste.

Roll the pastry out on a floured surface to ¼ inch thick; you want it to be sturdy. Cut into rectangles about 6 x 5 inches. Place the lamb mixture in a line about 1 inch in from one edge. Brush both edges with beaten egg, fold over the pastry, and press. I also fold the pastry back toward the filling (see photo opposite) to ensure it is well sealed.

Prick holes with a fork or slash at intervals with a knife. Brush once more with beaten egg to ensure the rolls turn nice and brown. Cut into 4-inch rolls. Bake for 25–30 minutes, until crisp. Serve hot or cold.

Spiced beef is a grand Cork Christmas tradition. I grew up nearby and we didn't have it locally at all, but my mother is from Cork and so I learned about it quickly. Brisket or top round is cured and spiced over a week or more, depending on the recipe. Different butchers have different recipes, but the spice flavor always smacks of Christmas. It has really interesting origins ... traders from Asia would travel to Cork's Butter Market—at the time the largest in Europe—and trade spices for butter. In Ireland we never made spiced beef, but bought it. This wasn't possible in London though, so I figured out quickly how to make it. You'll need to start the cure a good week before cooking the beef. Saltpeter, a preservative, can be difficult to find now as it is also used to make explosives(!), but you can source it online. Your butcher may give you some, too.

Spiced beef

Serves 8
4½ pounds beef brisket, off the bone

For the curing mix
1 teaspoon allspice
1 teaspoon cloves
1 teaspoon freshly grated nutmeg
1 teaspoon mace
¼ cup, plus 2 tablespoons soft brown sugar
2 teaspoons saltpeter
4 ounces sea salt

Combine all the ingredients for the curing mix and rub it all over the brisket. Sterilize a nonmetallic pot or plastic container into which the beef will fit snugly with boiling water. Add the beef, cover, and store in the refrigerator for eight days, turning daily and basting with juices.

Wipe off the excess marinade and cover the beef with water in a large saucepan. Bring to a boil and simmer gently for two hours.

Let cool and serve over the festive period thinly sliced, as you would a ham.

✦ LEFTOVERS ✦

Spiced beef toastie

This is simple and a bit of a guilty pleasure.

Slice spiced beef and a decent strong cheese such as cheddar. This makes a lovely Christmas snack, on toast, or in a toasted sandwich.

Spiced beef hash

The ultimate Christmas brunch.

Leftover potatoes fried with chunks of spiced beef and served with chopped flat-leaf parsley and a soft-fried egg will sooth any manner of overindulgence … and prepare you for the next lot.

Spiced beef mini pastries

Another great Christmas snack.

Tuck spiced beef with grated cheese in some folded store-bought puff pastry. Brush with beaten egg and bake for 10–15 minutes at 400°F until crisp.

✦ PASSION ✦

Gutsy ragu with gremolata

I am convinced that there are more opinions on ragu than on anything else in the world. Depending on who you talk to you're told never white wine, always red wine. Never use milk. It's a minefield. Whenever in doubt when it comes to Italian food I refer to Marcella Hazan, and Marcella says milk and white wine, so I tried that. And I liked it. The milk sweetens and the wine adds acidity, and that works for me. Always cook with a wine you would drink as, if you don't like the wine, you won't like your ragu.

Serves 6
For the ragu and pasta
3 carrots, quartered lengthwise and finely sliced
3 celery stalks, finely sliced
2 tablespoons light olive oil
3 garlic cloves, minced
2¼ pounds beef shin on the bone, meat removed and minced or ground
2 ounces bone marrow, scooped from the beef shin bone, minced
1¾ cups white wine
1¾ cups whole milk
3 bay leaves
2 x 14-ounce cans good tomatoes
sea salt
freshly ground black pepper
1 pound 10½ ounces pappardelle

For the gremolata
handful of flat-leaf parsley, chopped
4 garlic cloves, minced
finely grated zest of 1 unwaxed lemon

Saute the carrots and celery on medium-low heat for eight to 10 minutes, until softening. Add the garlic for a minute or so. Add the meat and bone marrow and brown with the vegetables. When browned, pour in the wine and boil off the alcohol over about two or three minutes. Add the milk and bay leaves, bring to a simmer, reduce the heat, and cook gently for three hours, stirring occasionally so it doesn't stick. Add the tomatoes when most of the liquid has evaporated. Season to taste. Cook the pappardelle according to package instructions. Combine the ingredients for the gremolata. Toss the ragu with the pappardelle. Serve with the gremolata on top.

Ragu and potato rolls

Follow the recipe for Lamb and Smoky Eggplant Rolls (see page 136), only substitute 10 ounces cooked potato, a handful of flat-leaf parsley, and 14 ounces ragu, roughly mashed together, as filling. Roll as instructed and brush with a beaten egg to ensure they get nice and brown when baked. Makes 4.

Ragu and potato cakes

Combine 9 ounces of leftover ragu with 1 pound 2 ounces mashed potatoes, ⅓ cup all-purpose flour, 2 shredded green onions, a handful of chopped flat-leaf parsley, and seasoning. Shape into balls and dip in seasoned flour, then in egg and finally in bread crumbs. Deep-fry until brown and crispy and serve on toothpicks as nibbles. Serves 4 as part of a spread.

Mini ragu pies

This doesn't require much instruction, or indeed any amounts. Preheat the oven to 350°F. Simply place leftover ragu in buttered or oiled small pie dishes and cover with a puff pastry lid. Brush the lid with beaten egg and bake for 20 minutes or so, until crisp.

Ragu and potato bake

Peel and finely slice 2¼ pounds potatoes with a mandolin. Add 5 tablespoons of heavy cream and mix with your hands to ensure that all slices are coated. Put three layers of potatoes in a buttered ovenproof dish, add a layer of ragu, and repeat until you have used all the potatoes, finishing with a layer of potatoes on top. Grate some Gruyère on top to finish and bake at 350°F for 30 minutes, until brown and crispy. Serves 4 with a green salad on the side.

People often throw away leftover pasta. I never do. It is delicious fried up the next day. That may sound wrong, but it really works. The Italians do it too, so it's worth a try, isn't it?

Ragu and pappardelle omelet

Serves 2
leftover pappardelle and ragu, as much as you have
2 eggs
handful of flat-leaf parsley, chopped
sea salt
freshly ground black pepper
1 tablespoon light oil

Combine all the ingredients except the oil and season with salt and pepper. Fry in the oil in a hot pan for 2–3 minutes, then put a plate on top, slide the omelet on to it, and flip it to cook on the other side. (Alternatively, finish it under the broiler for a couple of minutes until brown.) Serve in slices, as you would a tortilla, with some salad.

Empanadas are a lovely savory snack found all over South America. They are like a dumpling that has been wrapped with a heavier dough, so they are sturdier and crisper. Like a mini meat pie, really.

They are a perfect way to use up leftover ragu, especially if you don't have a lot left. Proper South American empanadas use a specific dough, but I find that simple pizza dough works very well here. Indeed, it's a perfect use for leftover pizza dough, which freezes very well. If you have any leftover, simply roll it out, and freeze pizza—or empanada—size sheets layered between wax paper. So, all those scraps of dough that you used to throw away? Don't, you never know when you can use them.

Ragu empanadas are rich, deeply savory, and delicious. Play around with the fillings: squash, spinach, chili, and goat cheese is a fantastic vegetarian version. Shredded chili chicken is a nice light meat filling. Any meaty leftovers with sauce, shredded (such as Spiced Slow-Roast Short Ribs, see page 124, or Slow-Cooked Pork Cheeks in Cider, see page 129) make a great empanada stuffing.

This recipe is just a guide, which is why there are no amounts; it's all about how much ragu you have leftover. So make as many as you can and enjoy them. These are great lunch fodder too, so don't be afraid to stick some in your lunchbox. Traditionally these are fried, as I do here. If you would prefer a healthier version, bake them in an oven preheated to 400°F for 12–15 minutes. Brush them with beaten egg if baking, so they turn a nice golden brown.

Ragu empanadas

leftover Pizza Dough, or make some fresh (see page 98)
leftover ragu, as much as you have
flat-leaf parsley
light oil, to fry

Roll your dough into thin 6-inch circles.

Put a couple of tablespoons of ragu filling, plus some parsley, into the center, brush the edges with water, and fold the dough over, creating a half-moon shape. Press the edges together then crimp them with a fork, ensuring they are tightly shut.

Heat about ½ inch of oil in a pan until a cube of bread froths the oil immediately when added. Fry the empanadas for two to three minutes on each side. Serve hot or cold. These are a perfect picnic snack.

Overnight shoulder of pork with spiced apple relish

This is a great weekend roast and special occasion dish and I've made it for Christmas, which gifted me a stress-free Christmas Day. The pork chugged away nicely on its own and left me with only a small amount to do on the day itself. A 12-hour roast results in meltingly tender pork you can pull apart with your fingers and sensational crackling. I add cider vinegar to the relish as I find its sharpness great with rich pork. It's sublime in a sandwich (with the meat and crackling) in a fluffy Irish blaa (see page 88). When thinking leftovers, think fennel, sage, lemon, beans, cabbage, and mustard.

Serves 8
8–9 pounds bone-in shoulder of pork, skin scored by your butcher
sea salt

For the spiced apple relish
6 baking apples
¼ cup cider vinegar
¼ cup superfine sugar
1 nutmeg
2 cinnamon sticks, broken up
1 red chili, chopped

Preheat the oven to 425°F. Boil a kettle of water and place the pork on a wire rack, skin side up, in the sink. Pour boiling water over the skin and drain. This puffs up the skin so it's ready to crackle. Wipe the skin bone dry with paper towels. Salt it with coarse sea salt. Roast for 20 minutes, cover with foil, and reduce the oven temperature to 250°F. Roast for 11 hours. Remove the foil, return the heat to 425°F, and roast for 10–15 minutes. You should have perfect crackling. Ensure you don't burn it at this stage and ruin all your hard work! Rest for at least 15 minutes. The pork will be so tender you can serve it with a spoon.

Meanwhile, peel and core the apples and boil with ¼ cup water, the vinegar, sugar, and spices until the apples are mushy. Serve with the spices still in.

Tip: the pork fat rendered out in the slow roasting process is terrific with roasted potatoes. Even better than goose fat, I say. Save it in a bowl or jar in your refrigerator.

I love this dish, shreds of pork mingling with—preferably—homecooked black beans (see page 160) and tomato is a delicious evening meal. It's great with rice, but I prefer to eat it with some toasted good bread.

Pork and black bean chili

Serves 2
1 tablespoon cumin seeds
1 red onion, minced
1 red chili, deseeded and minced
1 tablespoon olive oil
1 garlic clove, minced
14 ounces leftover pork shoulder, chopped
2 cups black beans (homecooked are best, see page 160), or
    14-ounce can black beans, drained and rinsed
1 tablespoon brown sugar
14-ounce can tomatoes
handful of cilantro leaves, chopped

Toast the cumin seeds over high heat in a dry pan. Grind with a mortar and pestle (or spice or coffee grinder) to a powder.

Sauté the onion and chili in the oil until soft. Add the garlic for the last minute.

Add the cumin, pork, the beans if homecooked, brown sugar, and tomatoes. Bring to a boil, reduce the heat, and simmer for 20 minutes. Add the beans, if canned, for the last five minutes.

Finish with the cilantro and it's ready to eat.

✦ LEFTOVERS ✦

Pork croquettes

Croquettes are lovely as a meal in themselves—think light lunch—but also great as a side to a big meal. The leftover pork will be really moist so won't need much assistance in sticking together.

Preheat the oven to 400°F. Season 1 pound 2 ounces of leftover pork shoulder, chopped. If it's a little dry (and it really shouldn't be), add a beaten egg, or as much of it as is needed to function as a glue. Shape into cylinders about 3 inches long and coat in seasoned flour, then beaten egg, and finally bread crumbs. Bake for 20 minutes, or deep-fry until crispy. Serves 2.

Pork and potato cakes with kale and an egg

How to improve the humble potato cake? Put pork in it! Delicious and cheap, it's a perfect speedy supper.

Mash 1 pound 2 ounces of boiled potatoes, add $1\frac{1}{2}$ tablespoons of unsalted butter, 2 tablespoons of all-purpose flour, a handful of flat-leaf parsley, chopped, and 10 ounces of leftover pork shoulder, shredded. Season to taste. If your potatoes were very fluffy you may need to add a beaten egg to hold the mixture together: try and form a patty and, if it won't hold, you will know you need to add one.

Fry the cakes in 1 tablespoon of light oil over medium heat for about five minutes on each side until warmed through. Serve with some lightly pan-fried kale or black leaf kale and a fried or poached egg. Be sure to keep that lovely yolk soft and allow it to dribble over the cake when you pierce it with your knife. Serves 4 as an appetizer or 2 as supper.

✦ PASSION ✦

Two- and six-hour pork belly

My obsession with pork belly became infamous in the early days of my blog. I am quite faddish with food anyway, developing love affairs with favorite ingredients before I overdose and need a break. I could write about The Pork Chronicles, The Chorizo Files, and a brief affair with dill from which I have never recovered. Pork belly has remained a keeper though. Who can resist that gorgeous rich flesh with its crackling cap? I can't.

Your choices here are determined by time. When I am hungry and impatient, I reach for the two-hour dish. When I have time, I love to let pork belly roast slowly, ideal for Sunday lunch when you put it in first thing. The cider-braised lentils are perfect with it.

Serves 4

4½-pound pork belly joint, skin scored by the butcher
sea salt
2 carrots, quartered lengthwise and sliced
1 celery stalk, finely sliced
1 shallot, minced
1 tablespoon light oil
11½ cups French green lentils
2 bay leaves
1½ cups hard cider
1½ cups light stock, such as chicken or pork

Preheat the oven to 450°F. Ensure your meat is at room temperature. Put the pork on a wire rack in your sink and pour boiling water over it. This puffs the skin and is one secret to good crackling. Dry the meat and skin thoroughly with paper towels. Just before you put it in the oven, and not a minute before, salt liberally with sea salt, rubbing it all over the joint. (If you do this too early it will ruin your crackling.) Put the pork in the oven for 15 minutes.

Reduce the oven temperature to 340°F and roast for 1½ hours, for two-hour pork, or to 250°F for 5½ hours for the six-hour version. Meanwhile, sauté the carrots, celery, and shallot in the oil for six to eight minutes. Take off the heat and mix with the lentils and bay leaves. Add to the pork with the cider and stock when the two-hour pork has 30 minutes left, or the six-hour pork has 1½ hours left. In both cases, return the oven to 450°F for a final 15 minutes to crisp the crackling, keeping an eye on it to ensure it doesn't burn.

Make dumpling wrappers (see page 56) or buy store-bought wonton wrappers or dumpling wrappers from Asian stores or large grocery stores.

Pork belly dumplings in broth

Serves 4
For the broth
pork or chicken bones, or chicken carcasses
2 tablespoons light oil
2 carrots, peeled and chopped
1 leek, washed and chopped
2–3 garlic cloves, whole, plus 2 more, minced
small handful of black peppercorns
1-inch chunk fresh gingerroot, minced
1 mild green chili, minced

For the dumplings
sea salt
freshly ground black pepper
1 pound 2 ounces leftover pork belly, shredded
5 ounces Chinese cabbage or other greens, shredded
20 dumpling wrappers
a few Chinese chives, chopped
3–4 greens onions, shredded

To make the broth, fry the bones in half the oil until caramelized, then place in a pot with the carrots, leek, whole garlic, and peppercorns. Cover with water and bring to a boil, scooping off any scum. Simmer for a couple of hours. Strain the broth and set aside.

Make the dumplings by putting 1 teaspoon of seasoned leftover pork belly and some shredded greens into a dumpling wrapper. Rub the edges with water and press closed. Make about five dumplings per person.

Sauté the ginger, green chili, and chopped garlic in the remaining oil for a minute or two. Add the broth and bring to a boil. Reduce the heat and add the dumplings. Cook for three or four minutes, no longer or they may burst.

Serve the broth and dumplings in bowls, sprinkling each with some Chinese chives and green onions.

Pork belly pancakes

I like to make this simple quick twist on Chinese duck pancakes. You will need to take a trip to the local Asian food store for the pancakes.

Steam the pancakes in a bamboo steamer or in a foil packet in your oven for 10 minutes, or according to the package instructions. Stuff them with shredded warmed leftover pork belly, shredded cucumber, and green onions and hoisin sauce. Scale the amounts up or down depending on how much leftover meat you have and how many mouths there are to feed. Serve as a snack or a hearty appetizer.

Pork, black leaf kale, and noodle soup

Make a broth as for the Pork Belly Dumplings in Broth (see opposite), adding the ginger, garlic, and chili, then similar amounts of leftover pork belly, shredded black leaf kale or regular kale, and a handful of egg or rice noodles. Cook for as long as the noodles require, season, and serve warm. Serves 4.

Crackling tips

No, this isn't leftovers, but I did tell you I was passionate about roast pork. This information is vital for fellow crackling lovers, and I had to fit it in somewhere!

Dry the skin! Whether through wiping with paper towels or using a hair dryer (I don't believe this is necessary, but some people swear by it).
Puff up the skin with boiling water to start the crackling off.
Salt just before you put it in the oven.
Only put dry spices and salt on the skin. Wet rubs will result in soggy skin.
Keep the heat high at the beginning and the end of cooking, watching as you go.

And a cheat. If you are still unhappy with your crackling—and you really shouldn't be, but just in case!—you can always crisp it under the broiler. But do take care as it is extremely easy to ruin all your hard work and burn it at this stage.

One chicken can go a very long way. Roast it and feast on the leftovers for a couple of days, or joint it for several meals. Jointing a chicken is easy and soon you'll be able to do it in minutes. Don't waste anything; everything from the skin to the carcass is delicious.

A perfect roast chicken requires a few things; it needs to be moist and flavorful and it needs to be crispy. The first place to start is with a good chicken; free-range organic are best, although free-range is the most important part.

Perfect roast chicken

Serves 4
1 chicken (about 2¼ pounds)
1 unwaxed lemon, halved
a few sprigs of thyme
4 garlic cloves
4 tablespoons unsalted butter
sea salt

Preheat the oven to 400°F. Remove the thick layer of fat from inside the chicken. This fat—known as shmaltz—is highly prized in Jewish cooking; save it for a batch of potatoes; it's delicious!

Put the lemon, thyme, and garlic in the cavity. Rub the butter into the skin generously, smothering it, and sprinkle over some sea salt.

Roast for 20 minutes, breast up. Reduce the oven temperature to 350°F. Turn the chicken breast down and roast for 25 minutes. Turn breast up again and roast for 25 minutes more.

Check that the chicken is cooked by pulling the leg away from the body; the juices should run clear. Continue to cook if you see traces of pink. Rest for 10 minutes for the juices to settle. Now it's ready to serve.

How to joint a chicken

A pair of poultry shears is a wise investment. Pull the legs away from the body. Cut around the leg then pull it from the body, releasing the joint from the socket by twisting. Split the leg and thigh by feeling for the space in the bone and cutting it with your shears.

Remove the wings by twisting at the joint and cutting to remove. Remove the breast meat by cutting away from you with a slim, flexible knife as close as you can to the carcass. Save the carcass for stock.

Peel off any extra skin and store it for skewers (see page 154).

Take the fat from inside the chicken and save for roasted potatoes.

This is a lovely, rustic, flavor-packed dish perfect for all year round; it's spritely in summer and comforting in winter. It also makes the best of the delicious chicken legs and thighs, which taste so much better than the breast. They are also way cheaper. Cooking chorizo is best here but dried is fine too, just don't buy the sliced stuff!

Roast chicken legs and thighs with tomato and chorizo

Serves 2
9 ounces chorizo
1 tablespoon light oil
2 garlic cloves, minced
14-ounce can diced tomatoes
1 tablespoon brown sugar
1 tablespoon olive oil
2 chicken thighs
2 chicken legs
sea salt
handful of flat-leaf parsley, chopped

Preheat the oven to 350°F.

Start the sauce by sautéing the chorizo in the light oil for four to five minutes over medium heat, until it has released its oils and is starting to crisp. Add the garlic for one minute. Add the tomatoes and sugar, reduce the heat, and cook for 10 minutes.

Place the tomato and chorizo sauce in an ovenproof dish that will fit the chicken. Rub the olive oil into the chicken skin, sprinkle it with salt, and place skin side up on the sauce.

Roast for 40 minutes. Check that the chicken is crisped and cooked through. It's ready when it is.

Sprinkle with the parsley and serve.

I love these; they are a real guilty pleasure and I eat them far too often. Chicken skin is such a treasure, I can't believe people throw it away! Years ago, when I was in Japan, I encountered one of the single best dishes I have ever eaten: a dish of gyoza dumplings wrapped in chicken skin, deep-fried, and served with thick, sweet Japanese mayonnaise. This was just one eating house among a throng of small, fantastic chicken grill places, hidden down alleys, where the American GIs once hung out after World War II. Different parts of the chicken are grilled on skewers over coals: innards, skin, thigh ... anything. I re-create these with chicken skin here. There aren't any amounts in this recipe, as it depends on how much chicken skin you can get your hands on!

Chicken skin skewers

wooden skewers
pinch of Chinese five spice
pinch of chili flakes
sea salt
chicken skin

Preheat the oven to 350°F. Soak the skewers in cold water for 20 minutes.

Rub the five spice, chili, and a little salt into the chicken skin. Wrap around the skewers and suspend the skewers over two opposite sides of an ovenproof dish, so none of the chicken skin is touching the dish.

Roast for 10 minutes, until crispy.

Who says it is expensive to eat well? This is the perfect use for leftover roast chicken. A carcass will contribute to a delicious fresh chicken stock and shredded leftover meat goes into the soup. It's also possible to make this with raw chicken meat, preferably thigh as it tastes much better and retains its moisture; although as it is a soup, breast meat will do fine, too.

This soup is wonderfully aromatic with lovely lemongrass, cilantro, and ginger to lift the soul. A little chili heat and some garlic complete the set. Thick rice noodles are my preference for this, although any noodles that you've got will do. You can even break up thin pasta and add it to the broth.

This recipe makes two big bowls for a filling supper. I would never want to eat this soup any other way.

Aromatic chicken noodle soup

Serves 2
2 lemongrass stalks, trimmed, halved lengthwise, and minced
1 red chili, deseeded and minced
1-inch chunk fresh gingerroot, minced
1 tablespoon light oil
2 garlic cloves, minced
10 ounces leftover chicken, shredded, or raw and sliced
3⅓ cups best chicken stock (homemade from the chicken carcass is best, see page 150)
5 ounces thick rice noodles, or egg noodles
sea salt
freshly ground black pepper
½ unwaxed lemon
handful of cilantro leaves

Fry the lemongrass, chili, and ginger in the oil for a couple of minutes over medium-high heat. Add the garlic and cook for 30 seconds.

Add the chicken and, if raw, fry until cooked on the outside (a couple of minutes). If cooked, just mix with the other ingredients.

Add the stock and cook for five minutes to let the flavors develop, then add the noodles and cook according to the package instructions (it should take no more than a few minutes).

Season and serve with a squeeze of lemon, scattered with cilantro.

Pumpkins and squashes are wonderful ingredients. Sweet in flavor, they go really well with intensely savory ingredients such as pancetta or ham. Soft, they love crispy things such as fried sage; gentle, they go well with strong aromas such as lemongrass. There are many varieties, shapes, and sizes. You can stuff and roast tiny squashes. I love to roast great big ones in wedges and do lots of different things with the resulting purée. Why roast? The roasting intensifies the flavor as the pumpkin loses water and you are left with a tastier and more manageable ingredient.

How to roast a pumpkin

First, tackle the pumpkin and cut it into more manageable chunks. It's easier to leave the skin on and worry about that later. You do need to take the seeds out though, which is very easy. Cut the pumpkin in half and scoop the seeds out with a spoon. (You can eat the seeds too; they're delicious roasted and salted once you have removed them from the stringy flesh.) I usually cut large round pumpkins into six or eight wedges, and long squashes like butternut into two.

To roast, place the wedges skin side down on an oiled baking sheet and roast in a preheated oven at 350°F until soft.

Use immediately as a side dish with spiced olive oil, or peel and store any extra in the refrigerator for three days, or in the freezer.

What to do with your roasted pumpkin? Read on…

Roast pumpkin and chili soup

This is a lovely warming soup that is super-quick when you've got your pumpkin prepared already.

Sauté one minced onion in 1 tablespoon of light oil for six to eight minutes, until starting to soften; add 2 minced garlic cloves, 1-inch chunk minced fresh gingerroot, and 2 minced green chilies for two minutes. Add 3⅓ cups chicken or vegetable stock, ½ cup red lentils, 1 pound 2 ounces roast pumpkin, and scant 1 cup coconut milk. Bring to a boil, reduce the heat, and cook gently for 15 minutes. Add a handful of cilantro leaves, blend, and season to taste. Serve while warm. Serves 4 for a light lunch, or 2 for a generous supper.

Pumpkin, goat cheese, spinach, and chili rolls

These were another market stall favorite. A great vegetarian dish, meat eaters will love them too.

For a fresh vegetarian roll, simply make sausage rolls as for the Lamb and Smoky Eggplant Rolls (see page 136), but fill them with goat cheese, wilted spinach, and some roast pumpkin. The filling ingredients should together weigh 1⅓ pounds– 1 pound 9 ounces, though the balance is up to you; use more cheese for a tangier roll, or more pumpkin for extra sweetness and season it well. Sprinkle with chili flakes for some heat and roll, brush the pastry with beaten egg, and bake as in the lamb recipe. Makes 4.

I first had pumpkin gnocchi many years ago when a friend's father in Naples made them for us for lunch. I was hooked immediately and they have been on the menu ever since.

Pumpkin gnocchi are a little tricky to make but, once you get the hang of them, really quick and delicious. You can have a great meal in minutes. There are a few things that you must pay attention to:

Ensure that the pumpkin is roasted until just soft, so that it retains its structure and is not too wet. If the pumpkin is really wet, let it drain through a strainer for a few hours. It may seem extreme but it makes a huge difference.

Work the flour in gently and quickly. If you overwork—and this can happen in just minutes—it will become gloopy and unpleasant.

Don't worry that they are difficult to shape by hand, unlike potato gnocchi. This is the way they are; they're a little messier and very light. Also don't worry about making pretty fork shapes or anything like that. They're too soft.

To make your life that much easier, instead of rolling by hand, pipe them into the water using a disposable pastry bag, cutting them with scissors into the right size as you pipe them out, and letting them drop into the pan.

Pumpkin gnocchi with sage brown butter

Serves 2

1 pound 2 ounces roasted pumpkin, mashed (see page 156)
scant 1 cup all-purpose flour, plus more to dust
generous grating of nutmeg
sea salt
freshly ground black pepper
8 tablespoons unsalted butter
about 12 sage leaves
Parmesan cheese, to serve (optional)

Spread the mashed pumpkin out on a tray or cutting board. Sift over the flour and add the nutmeg and some salt and pepper. Gently combine the flour with the pumpkin using a fork until there are no traces of white. The dough should be starting to come together. Place in a pastry bag (see recipe introduction) or gently, with floured hands, shape them into rolls, and cut gnocchi at 1-inch sections along it.

Cook in simmering water for four to five minutes.

Meanwhile, melt the butter with the sage leaves, which will crisp as they fry. Serve the gnocchi in the melted butter with the crispy sage, shaving a little Parmesan over the top, if you like.

Homecooked beans

Homecooked beans are a passion of mine. Canned beans are often flaccid and depressing; swollen with salt and water they can be tasteless. Homecooked beans are a world away. They have great texture and flavor; sure they take time, but it's not time in which you're actually doing anything; you are just leaving them to soak or simmer. Other advantages are that they are very cheap and, frozen in 2-cup batches, make your cooking life very convenient.

One thing to note about homecooked beans is that they need to be relatively fresh, even when dried, or they will take forever to cook, if at all. Source them well in good stores or delis. I never cook beans with anything else, preferring to cook them separately, drain them and only then add them to what I am cooking.

Never salt beans either before or during cooking, as the salt will cause a reaction that toughens the skins. You want beautifully yielding beans, not little bullets.

Soak your beans overnight if you can, or for a minimum of six hours. Not all beans need it, but some do as they contain nasty substances that can make you ill (red kidney beans, especially, contain chemicals that will make you very ill unless soaked out). Besides, it's worth doing as all beans will cook better after soaking.

For all beans, after soaking, drain them, cover with fresh water, and bring to a boil. Scoop off any scum that rises to the top, reduce the temperature, and cook until the beans soften. For most this will be between 30 and 90 minutes.

All of the following recipes assume that the beans are cooked already.

This is a great hearty, gutsy dish. Homecooked beans are in themselves quite meaty and, combined with the sausages and tomato sauce, make a great, quick dish for any time of the day. Leftovers can be served up at breakfast time, with eggs.

Navy bean and sausage casserole

Serves 4

1 red onion, minced
1 tablespoon olive oil
10 ounces good-quality sausages, chopped
2 garlic cloves, minced
14-ounce can diced tomatoes
2 cups cooked navy beans (homemade are best, see opposite)
1 heaping cup light chicken or vegetable stock
handful of flat-leaf parsley, chopped

Sauté the onion in the oil until soft over medium heat. Add the sausages and stir until brown on all sides. Add the garlic and cook for only a minute.

Add the tomatoes, beans, and stock, stir, cover, and cook for 15 minutes. Sprinkle with the parsley and serve warm.

This is a lovely protein-packed alternative to mashed potatoes, perfect for healthier days on weeks where carbs have already featured heavily. The garlic and rosemary here lend the dish a lovely Mediterranean feel and give the otherwise dull white beans a lift.

Garlic and rosemary cannellini bean mash

Serves 1
1 garlic clove, minced
2 tablespoons extra virgin olive oil
1 teaspoon minced rosemary
2 cups cooked cannellini beans
    (homemade are best, see page 160)
sea salt
freshly ground black pepper

Sauté the garlic in the extra virgin olive oil with the rosemary for a minute. Add all of the oil, rosemary, and garlic to the beans.

Mash lightly with a fork, keeping it quite chunky. Season with salt and pepper to taste.

Black beans are the best beans for burgers, as they are the meatiest and have a dense texture that holds together quite well. Don't be put off by memories of the soggy, flaccid, depressed relatives of these that are commonly found in takeout restaurants. These are sturdy and full-flavored and you might find the meat eaters clamoring for them, too.

Spiced bean burgers

Makes 4
1 teaspoon cumin seeds
2 garlic cloves, minced
1 tablespoon light oil, plus more to fry
4 cups cooked black beans
   (homemade are best, see page 160)
½ teaspoon chili flakes
1 cup bread crumbs
handful of cilantro leaves, chopped
1 egg, beaten

Dry-fry the cumin seeds in a small frying pan until they are aromatic and have darkened a shade. Grind to a powder in a mortar and pestle.

Fry the garlic in the oil for a minute, or until aromatic. Pour the beans into a large bowl and add the garlic and oil from the pan and all the other ingredients.

Shape the mixture into four patties and fry for about five minutes on each side over medium heat until brown.

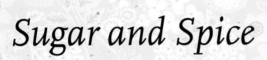

Sugar and Spice

When it comes to desserts—and sweet things generally—I always lean toward fruit. I love it. I like desserts that are light and, while I occasionally slip toward death by sugar and butter territory, I like to be able to get up from the dinner table afterward and carry on with my day. I also like desserts to be fairly quick to make, although I have a few more detailed recipes here, such as Raspberry and Rose Ripple Ice Cream (see page 174).

Childhood memories of blackberries, rhubarb, gooseberries, and apples permeate my sweet consciousness, as does my obsession with lemon curd, which has somewhat evolved. I've always adored meringue pies and think they're terribly underrated, while my passion for the simple éclair knows no bounds. I first tried to make choux pastry when I was too young to be wielding a hot pan, such was my desperation to have one. Living in the countryside nowhere near a store forces resourcefulness and creativity!

My mother always endeavored to get me to drink milk or eat any dairy as a child, but outside of desserts and yogurts I wasn't at all interested. Then I discovered gooseberry and rhubarb fools made with yogurt and cream and I was sold. It's not quite healthy, but the compromise was enough for my mother to concede and allow my indulgence. I was a tiny thing then and my body could take the calorie load. I am not so fortunate now, but I do indulge occasionally. You just have to, don't you?

Quinces are fantastic, aromatic with delicate perfume. They're wonderful in season and also available jarred all year round. (If you use jarred, omit the boiling stage here.)

There are dedicated tarte Tatin pans, and it is best to use one, but if you don't have one, use an 8-inch ovenproof frying pan. I use store-bought puff pastry, as the all-butter stuff is really good and there's no need to put yourself through the trauma of making it.

Rosehips in season are bountiful but, if they are out of season, you can source dried hips easily online from beer brewing websites. They are packed with Vitamin C, a bonus!

If you can't face making sorbet, this is delicious with vanilla crème fraîche, too. Just scrape the seeds from half a vanilla bean into a pot of crème fraîche and stir.

Quince tarte Tatin with rosehip sorbet

Serves 4

For the rosehip sorbet
5 ounces dried rosehips, crushed
   (or double that amount, fresh)
1⅛ cups superfine sugar
juice of 1 unwaxed lemon

For the tarte Tatin
4 quinces
¾ cup superfine sugar
1 pound 2 ounces all-butter
   puff pastry
8 tablespoons (1 stick) unsalted butter

Bring the rosehips and sugar to a boil with 3¾ cups water. When the sugar dissolves, remove from the heat and let cool. Strain and add the lemon when cold. For best results, churn in an ice-cream maker. If you don't have one, put in the freezer in a covered container. After an hour, whisk. Repeat every 30 minutes. It should be ready after two hours.

Preheat the oven to 375°F. Peel the quinces and cut into ½-inch wedges. I take the seeds out but, if you prefer the quinces to be pink, leave them in until cooked. Place in a saucepan, cover with water, and add ¼ cup of the sugar. Bring to a boil and cook until tender (about 20 minutes). Drain. Remove the seeds and cores, if you left them in.

Roll the pastry to ¼ inch thick and large enough to cover your pan. Prick with a fork all over and keep in the refrigerator until you need it.

Caramelize the butter and remaining sugar in a saucepan by melting gently until golden brown. Be careful not to burn it. Arrange the quinces in the pan to cover the bottom, then pour the caramel over. Cook for 15 minutes to allow to caramelize, then cover with the pastry. Cook for 30 minutes, until golden and crisp. Serve warm with the sorbet.

Tip: if you leave the seeds in the quinces while boiling, they go a little pink. Leave them out, they stay yellow! Up to you, whichever you prefer.

✦ PASSION ✦

Blackberry and crème fraîche phyllo tart

This is one of the desserts from my market stall, made when blackberries were in season. It's very simple, layers of crispy phyllo with crème fraîche, berries, mint, and honey between. Baked until crisp, it's a terrific late summer dessert. It's also very quick with store-bought phyllo. There is really no need to make phyllo pastry at home.

Serves 4–6
9 tablespoons butter, plus more for the pan
2 cups crème fraîche
2¾ cups blackberries
¼ cup honey
about 12 mint leaves, shredded
9-ounce package phyllo pastry

Butter an 8-inch square ovenproof dish, and preheat the oven to 350°F.

Combine the crème fraîche, blackberries, honey, and mint. Mix gently; you don't want to crush the blackberries too much.

Divide the phyllo sheets into four groups. Place the first layer on the bottom of the dish, brushing each layer generously with melted butter.

Put one-third of the crème fraîche and blackberry mix on top. Cover with the next layer of phyllo and repeat until there are four layers of phyllo and three of filling, ensuring each phyllo sheet is brushed with butter.

Bake for 15–20 minutes, until the phyllo is crisp. Eat warm or cold.

Another market favorite, I made these cute little tarts in muffin pans. The recipe is relatively quick as it uses store-bought phyllo and is really fresh and delicious. This tart is especially good with Homemade Ricotta (see page 70) that has been drained so it is quite firm. If you are using store-bought ricotta, drain it, as it can be a bit too wet.

Raspberry and ricotta tarts

Serves 6
1¼ cups ricotta (homemade is best, see page 70)
1 egg
5 tablespoons heavy cream
¼ cup superfine sugar
12 mint leaves, minced
9 ounces phyllo pastry
10 tablespoons unsalted butter, melted
scant 2½ cups raspberries

Drain the ricotta in a strainer or a bundle of cheesecloth until it has lost most of its moisture. Preheat the oven to 350°F.

Combine the ricotta with the egg, cream, and sugar and whip with a mixer or electric whisk until smooth. Add the mint leaves and stir through until evenly distributed.

Butter a six-cup muffin pan. Cut the phyllo into 6-inch squares and put four layers in each cup, buttering each as you go. Arrange the layers so that you get lots of edges pointing out at the top.

Divide the ricotta mixture between the tartlets and bake for 15–20 minutes, until the pastry is a crisp brown.

Let cool slightly, then arrange the raspberries on top. Serve cool.

Candying fruit is an ancient way of preserving it; driving out the water and replacing it with sugars makes it last so much longer. Candied orange zests dipped in chocolate are an old French candy that still taste great today. Make a large batch of them and store in an airtight jar for emergencies.

Orangettes

Makes 30–35
2 large oranges
¾ cup sugar
4 ounces best semisweet chocolate

Peel the oranges from top to bottom, ensuring the zest comes off in strips. Scrape off and discard any white pith that clings to the zest. Cut the zest into equal widths of about ¼ inch.

Bring a saucepan of water to a boil, add the orange zest strips, and boil for a few minutes to remove any bitterness. Drain.

Make a stock syrup by heating the sugar and ⅔ cup water until the sugar is dissolved. Bring to a boil. Add the zest strips, bring to a boil again, reduce the heat, cover, and simmer for an hour or so, taking care to ensure that the zest strips are covered with syrup at all times. Drain and let cool.

Melt the chocolate in a heatproof bowl over gently simmering water, making sure the bowl does not touch the water. Dip in the candied strips so that half of each is covered in chocolate. Place on a wire rack to drain, with a piece of wax paper underneath to catch the drips.

Let cool and they are ready to serve. Perfect with tea or coffee, or as a sneaky snack.

This really simple and delicious recipe is deliberately dairy free, so it's perfect for those that are lactose intolerant or dairy allergic. It's also relatively guilt free. Good chocolate is actually quite good for you, as long as you are not eating it by the truckload.

I learned the mousse recipe in school and made it obsessively when younger. There are raw eggs here but don't be afraid of that, source them well and all is good. This is the way chocolate mousse was always made. As there are only two ingredients in it, make sure you use really good chocolate and really good eggs; you will taste the quality.

The honeycomb recipe is very easy but takes a little care. Do invest in a sugar or jam thermometer and watch it. If it looks like it is getting too dark, it is burning, so take it off the heat. Use a high-sided pan as, when you add the baking soda, the sugar will go crazy and rise to several times its size. This is also the step where you are most likely to burn yourself, so do take care. Those warnings aside it's a really fun thing to make, so do try it and enjoy it. Any leftovers make terrific homemade candy, covered in dark chocolate.

Chocolate mousse with honeycomb

Serves 6

For the mousse
6½ ounces best semisweet
   chocolate
6 eggs, separated

For the honeycomb
light oil, for the pan
1½ cups superfine or granulated sugar
½ cup light corn syrup
1 tablespoon cider or white wine vinegar
2 heaping teaspoons baking soda

First make your honeycomb. Prepare a pan or heatproof dish by lining with lightly oiled parchment paper. Heat the sugar, syrup, ⅓ cup water, and vinegar until it turns amber and reaches 300°F (the "hard crack" stage). Add the baking soda and stir well, then pour into your lined pan. Let cool to room temperature. If you want it in ordered shapes, cut with an oiled knife when it's nearly at room temperature. I like it to look a little rough and tumble, so cut it when it's cool.

For the mousse, break the chocolate into squares and melt gently in a double boiler, or in a saucepan over another saucepan of simmering water, until melted. Meanwhile, whisk the egg whites until stiff.

Once the chocolate is melted, remove from the heat and whisk in the egg yolks (they will cook if you keep them on the heat; you don't want scrambled egg in your mousse). When combined, gently add the egg whites, taking care not to knock out any of the air you have whisked in. Don't worry too much if it doesn't look very mousselike at this stage, it will be lovely when it's set. Pour into your serving glasses and leave in the refrigerator for two hours. Serve with honeycomb shards on top.

✦ PASSION ✦

Orange and cardamom jello with clotted cream

Ice cream and jello was a favorite childhood dessert and I still love to have it, although now I eat more grown-up versions. I do love jello on its own, especially with more adult flavors such as spices involved, but I love to serve this one with clotted cream, that wonderful rich preserved cream. Orange and cardamom is a very festive ice cream, but works well all year round. Again, it's a ridiculously easy dessert.

Serves 6
8 cardamom pods
4 cups fresh orange juice (about 10 oranges, depending on size)
finely grated zest and juice of 2 unwaxed lemons
¼ cup superfine sugar
2 x ¼-ounce envelopes granulated gelatin
clotted cream, to serve

Bruise the cardamom pods with the back of a knife and add to the citrus juices, lemon zest, and sugar in a saucepan. Bring just to a boil, then take off the heat. Let sit for 15 minutes to let the cardamom infuse.

Meanwhile, soak the gelatin in a small amount of cold water according to the package instructions for 5–10 minutes.

After 15 minutes, while the juice is still warm, strain it through a strainer. Add the gelatin to the warmed, strained juice and stir to dissolve.

Pour the juice into six individual glasses, leaving room on top for a spoon of clotted cream. Let chill and set in the refrigerator for four to six hours. Serve cold with the clotted cream on top.

Crème brûlée is a relatively simple and impressive dessert. It's just a baked custard with a caramelized sugar crust on top. Simple! It's like making the custard for an ice cream (see page 174) so once you've conquered one, be sure to try the other. I make homemade pistachio nut butter to give this a lovely twist. Make extra nut butter and save it in the refrigerator to spread on toast for very quick breakfasts.

You will need to make these in advance to allow them to set. For a little extra drama, caramelize the sugar on top with a cook's blowtorch.

Pistachio crème brûlée

Serves 4
For the brûlées
2 cups heavy cream
¼ cup, plus 2 tablespoons superfine sugar, plus 8 teaspoons for topping
1 teaspoon vanilla extract
4 large egg yolks

For the pistachio nut butter
⅔ cup shelled unsalted pistachios
1 teaspoon sea salt
1 tablespoon peanut oil

Preheat the oven to 300°F.

Heat the cream and sugar over medium heat until just before it boils. Add the vanilla and remove from the heat. Let cool for 10 minutes.

Make your nut butter by blending the pistachios with the salt, adding as much of the oil as you need to get a firm butter. Don't purée completely; it's best to leave some chunks in.

In a bowl, beat the egg yolks until frothy. Slowly add the cooled cream mixture, whisking as you do. It's important that you add it slowly so it doesn't cook the eggs. Strain the mixture to remove any stringy bits which may have formed.

Pour into four ramekins and place in a deep roasting pan. Stir 1 tablespoon of the nut butter into each to make a ripple effect. Pour boiling water from a kettle into the pan so that it comes halfway up each ramekin. Bake for half an hour, or until set but have a slight wobble. Let cool and chill in the refrigerator for at least two hours, or overnight. When ready to serve, sprinkle about 2 teaspoons of sugar on top of each and put under the broiler until caramelized, or torch with a cook's blowtorch.

My childhood memories of ice cream are fierce. My grandfather always had a supply in his freezer and when we were good we were allowed a slice between wafers. Once, when tiny, I refused to eat my lunch of a huge and intimidating pile of mashed potatoes with lots of peas which I loathed. My grandmother wouldn't cave and nor would I. So I sat for what seemed like an eternity watching my cousins playing out the window. Eventually, my grandfather whisked me out, gave me some ice cream, and put me out in the backyard where my grandmother wouldn't see me eat the forbidden treat.

My favorite, then and now, was raspberry ripple. I love to add rose now. Rose and raspberries are terrific together and make the ice cream that much more elegant.

Homemade ice cream is a little finicky but worth the trouble, especially for creating unusual flavors that you can't buy. It will also taste better (of course!). You can make it by hand by taking it out of the freezer every 30 minutes or so and whisking, but I say an ice-cream machine is a worthwhile and great-value investment.

Raspberry and rose ripple ice cream

Makes about 1.5 quarts
For the ice cream
1 vanilla bean
2½ cups heavy cream
2½ cups whole milk
1 cup superfine sugar
6 large egg yolks

For the raspberry and rose ripple
3¼ cups raspberries
¼ cup superfine sugar
2 tablespoons rosewater

Halve the vanilla bean and scrape the seeds into the cream and milk in a saucepan. Add the bean and sugar and bring to a gentle simmer. When the sugar has dissolved, take it from the heat and remove the vanilla bean (the seeds will remain). Whisk the egg yolks until they thicken. Slowly add the cream, initially in only a trickle so as not to scramble the yolks. Put the custard into a pan over very low heat, stirring so it doesn't burn. After 15 minutes it should coat the back of a spoon. Put in a bowl and cover. Cool, stirring to prevent a skin from forming.

Once it has cooled, churn in an ice-cream machine. Meanwhile, bring the raspberries, ¼ cup water, and the sugar to a boil and cook until it reduces to a sticky sauce; about five minutes. Add your rosewater. Intensify the flavor by reducing a little further and your ripple is done. If you don't like seeds, strain it, but I like to keep them in. Add some of the churned ice cream to a freezer container, then some of the ripple, then repeat until it's all in there. Use a palette knife to ripple it through. Freeze, or serve immediately.

✦ PASSION ✦

Chili chocolate truffles

Chocolate truffles are gorgeous, a perfect petit four at the end of a meal. Sinfully rich and ridiculously easy, I find that a gentle chili heat raises the bar. Use the best chocolate you can get as this is the primary flavor. Bad chocolate = bad truffles. I add a little salt as it goes so well with the chocolate. People won't even know that it is in there; it is very subtle.

Makes about 20
1 heaping cup heavy cream
pinch of sea salt
4 tablespoons unsalted butter
1 red chili, halved and deseeded
9 ounces semisweet chocolate (at least 70% cocoa solids), grated or minced
½ cup unsweetened cocoa powder, sifted

In a saucepan, heat the cream, salt, and butter gently with the chili, until it starts to move. Don't boil it.

Remove it from the heat, remove the chili, and add the chocolate, stirring to melt. Let it cool, then to solidify in the refrigerator. Overnight is easiest, but for at least four hours.

Scoop out a teaspoonful at a time and roll gently in the cocoa powder. They are ready to eat.

I first had cakes like these in one of my favorite ice-cream stores in London, Gelupo. As I took a bite I thought, WOW, I've got to try and make these at home. So I did. They contain olive oil in place of butter and make a really good snack with a cup of tea or coffee. These are gorgeous with blood oranges in season, but normal oranges are fine.

Little polenta, almond, and blood orange cakes

Makes about 12, depending on the size of your molds
2 tablespoons honey
2 whole blood oranges, peeled, in ½-inch dice
1 heaping cup all-purpose flour, plus more for the pan
1 tablespoon baking powder
pinch of sea salt
1½ cups cornmeal
1 cup ground almonds
¼ cup, plus 2 tablespoons superfine sugar
3 eggs, separated
juice from 4 blood oranges and finely grated zest of 1
1 cup olive oil, plus more for the pan
confectioners' sugar, to dust (optional)

Preheat the oven to 350°F. Combine the honey with the diced oranges and set aside while you prepare and bake the cakes. This will create a lovely syrup for the top.

Sift the flour, baking powder, and salt into a mixing bowl and stir in the cornmeal, almonds, and sugar.

Whisk together the egg yolks, orange juice, zest, and oil and stir through the flour mixture gently, keeping the air that you have sifted in.

Whisk the egg whites until fluffy as you would for meringue (this makes the cakes lovely and light). Fold gently through the other ingredients. Bake in a lightly oiled and floured cupcake pan for 40 minutes, until they spring back to the touch.

Remove and cool on a wire rack. Serve with the blood oranges and honey poured over the top. Dust with confectioners' sugar, if you like.

✦ PASSION ✦

Elderflower and gooseberry fool

Gooseberries are a wonderful fruit; I think I loved them even more as I was the only child in the house that liked them so I had them all to myself. My aunt grew them in her fruit patch and I would pick them, wondering if they would be too sour, or gone too far and then too sweet and lacking in flavor. I was never sure and, when I hit one that was right, I would devour more.

The tart gooseberries work very well with cream in a gooseberry fool; let's face it, what doesn't? Elderflower is a perfect match for it, too. I make my fool simply with whipped cream for a quick and simple summer dessert. If you want to make it more of a breakfast dish, mix the gooseberries with Greek yogurt instead of cream, or use half and half for a more health-conscious dessert.

Serves 4
14 ounces gooseberries, trimmed
⅓ cup elderflower cordial
about ¼ cup superfine sugar (depends on how tart
your gooseberries are, so taste to check)
2 cups heavy cream, lightly whipped

Cook the gooseberries with the elderflower cordial and sugar until soft and mushy. Taste to ensure it is sweet enough, though bear in mind that the taste will be muted a bit by the cream.

Let the gooseberries cool and stir gently through the cream to create a marbled effect. Spoon into individual glasses and serve chilled.

✦ PASSION ✦

Two curds, but I can't help it. It's important to make curd in a double boiler, or improvise one with a saucepan sitting over another filled with simmering water. This allows the curd to cook in a gentler fashion and ensures, with regular stirring, that the eggs don't turn into an omelet. Both these curds will keep for two weeks in the refrigerator.

Curd is wonderful on sourdough toast. It also makes a terrific fruit fool; stirred into cream cheese it is a cheesecake topping; or with broken meringues, cream, and blueberries.

Rhubarb and blood orange curd

Makes 2 small jars
7 ounces rhubarb, trimmed and chopped
4 tablespoons unsalted butter
¼ cup superfine sugar
finely grated zest of 1 blood orange and juice of 2
2 whole eggs, plus 2 egg yolks

Preheat the oven to 300°F. Roast the rhubarb for 15 minutes, until tender. Drain in a strainer. Meanwhile, melt the butter and sugar in a double boiler. Add the zest, juice, eggs, and yolks and cook gently, stirring. When it coats the back of a spoon, take it from the heat. Stir through the rhubarb. Store in a covered bowl or jars.

Passion fruit and lime curd

Makes 2 small jars
6 tablespoons unsalted butter
¼ cup, plus 2 tablespoons superfine sugar
3 passion fruits, seeds and pulp scraped out
finely grated zest and juice of 1 lime
2 whole eggs, plus 2 egg yolks

Melt the butter and sugar in a double boiler. Add the passion fruit seeds and pulp, zest, juice, eggs, and yolks. Cook gently, stirring, until the curd coats the back of a spoon. It will thicken as it cools. Store in a covered bowl or jars.

I love meringue pie, it's utterly comforting, nostalgic, and just beautiful to eat. It's especially nice in January, after an endless parade of green and brown food, when the gorgeous Yorkshire forced rhubarb and bright blood oranges arrive. If you can't get blood oranges, feel free to substitute normal oranges.

Lots of meringue pie recipes call for cornstarch to thicken the curd, but I prefer not to use it here. Some time in the refrigerator will allow it all to set. The results are a little sloppier than the traditional version perhaps, but the flavor is terrific.

Rhubarb and blood orange meringue pie

Makes a 10-inch tart
For the sweet piecrust pastry
6 tablespoons unsalted butter, chilled and diced
1 heaping cup all-purpose flour, sifted, plus more to dust
¼ cup confectioners' sugar, sifted
1 egg yolk, lightly beaten with the same amount of water

For the filling
1 x quantity Rhubarb and Blood Orange Curd (see page 179)

For the meringue
3 egg whites
½ cup confectioners' sugar, sifted
scant ¼ cup cornstarch

To make the pastry, add the butter to the flour and confectioners' sugar and rub it in with your fingertips until it looks like crumbs. Add the egg to bring together, mold into a ball, wrap, and chill for an hour.

Preheat the oven to 350°F. Roll the pastry out until big enough to line a 10-inch pie dish. Line with parchment paper, fill with baking beans, and blind bake for 20–25 minutes. Increase the oven temperature to 400°F. Pour the curd into the shell.

Whisk the egg whites until starting to form stiff peaks, add half the sugar, whisk again, then sift in the cornstarch and gently fold in with the remaining sugar. Spoon the meringue on top of the curd, trying to create lots of little peaks that will brown and ensuring it touches the pastry edge. Bake for five minutes or so, until starting to brown.

Let the tart cool and the curd to set for a couple of hours in the refrigerator. Serve cold. Try not to eat it all in one sitting, as I have done!

I remember baking an apple in school and being amazed at the results. I immediately started to calculate how many I could make from the apple tree down the road. A lot! I tired of it pretty quickly as I overindulged, but I do love making this simple, flavorful, and healthy dessert as an adult.

Our school recipe had lots of dried fruit. I prefer to keep these simple, adding cinnamon, sugar, and butter to the inside. I use baking apples.

Baked apple

Serves 4
4 baking apples
4 teaspoons Calvados
4 teaspoons brown sugar
1 teaspoon ground cinnamon
4 teaspoons unsalted butter, plus more for the baking pan

Preheat the oven to 350°F.

Core the apple and, halfway down each, cut a fine line across its equator through the skin to the flesh. This will ensure that the apple won't burst. A handy tip!

Put 1 teaspoon of Calvados in each apple followed by 1 teaspoon of sugar and a pinch of cinnamon. Finish with 1 teaspoon of butter.

Put the apples in a buttered baking pan and pour some water in, just enough to cover the bottom of the pan. Bake for 45–50 minutes, until the apples are soft. Serve hot as they are, or with some Greek yogurt on top.

Baked cheesecake brings back memories of a birthday in Paris. We took the Eurostar at stupid o'clock and spent the night. After spending an enthusiastic day walking and walking, and eating and eating, I could hardly move by sunset. My birthday meal was predominantly a battle with my eyelids, which were determined to close.

The next day, a wander around the Marais revealed the wonder of baked ricotta cheesecake in an Orthodox Jewish bakery. I had a slice there and took another for the Eurostar journey home. It has been a favorite ever since. I like to make it slightly differently with lemon and blueberry to give it a bit of a spritz.

Lemon and blueberry ricotta cheesecake

Serves 6
2 cups ricotta (homemade is best, see page 70)
4 eggs
scant 1 cup superfine sugar
1/3 cup all-purpose flour, sifted
juice of 2 unwaxed lemons
2/3 cup blueberries
unsalted butter, for the pan

Preheat the oven to 300°F.

Whisk the ricotta, eggs, and sugar until frothy. Add the flour and lemon juice and whisk until smooth. Stir in the blueberries gently.

Butter an 8-inch cake pan and pour in the batter. Bake for 30 minutes. Check that the cake is set in the center—it should be—but if it's not give it a few more minutes.

Let cool and served sliced.

This will accentuate any table and refresh on a hot summer's day. The rosewater is subtle, you want a gentle flavor not the sensation of drinking perfume.

Cucumber and rosewater

Serves 4
1 cucumber, cut into long strips with a vegetable peeler
petals from 1 organic rose
1 tablespoon rosewater

Combine all the ingredients in a glass pitcher—you will want to show off this drink—with 4 cups of water and lots of ice. Serve immediately.

Really refreshing; lovely on a sunny afternoon, with a spicy Shrimp Curry (see page 41).

Mango and mint lassi

Serves 4
2 mangos
2½ cups yogurt (homemade is best, see page 12)
1¾ cups whole milk
handful of fresh mint leaves, shredded

Purée the mangos, yogurt, and milk. Add the mint and stir through. Refrigerate until you want to serve it.

Chili may seem odd in a drink but mild chili has a gentle kick which, against ice, gives a lovely hot-cold sensation. Lemongrass gives aroma and sweet mandarin loves it all.

Mandarin, chili, and lemongrass juice

Serves 4
1 pound 10½ ounces mandarins, juiced
1 lemongrass stalk, trimmed and minced
½ mild red chili, deseeded and minced

Blend all the ingredients until you can no longer see any chunks of lemongrass and only flecks of chili remain. Serve with lots of ice.

Rosehip and lemon martini

Makes 1
¼ cup gin (I like Hendricks as it has rose notes which work well here)
2 tablespoons vermouth
1 teaspoon rosehip syrup
squeeze of unwaxed lemon, plus a lemon twist to serve

The glamorous bit! Add all the liquids to a cocktail shaker (or jam jar if you're stuck) with ice, and strain to serve with your dapper lemon twist.

Rhubarb and rose bellini

Makes 5
12 ounces rhubarb, chopped
2 tablespoons superfine sugar (unnecessary for forced rhubarb)
up to 2 tablespoons rosewater
1 bottle of prosecco, chilled

Preheat the oven to 350°F. Roast the rhubarb for 15 minutes, until soft. Stir in the sugar to dissolve, if needed, and cool.

Add the rosewater in teaspoons and check the flavor. Early season, pink, sweet (particularly forced) rhubarb won't need much; midsummer greener rhubarb—extraordinarily tart at times—may need more.

Put 2 teaspoons of this compote into five champagne flutes. Top off with chilled prosecco, stir, and serve immediately.

Elderflower bellini

Makes 5
For the bellini
1 bottle prosecco, chilled

For the elderflower cordial
½ cup superfine sugar
12 heads of elderflowers
1 unwaxed lemon, cut in half

Dissolve the sugar in 3 cups water. Cool. Add the elderflowers. Squeeze in the lemon and add its shell. Refrigerate to infuse for a couple of days. Strain and refrigerate.

To make the bellini, add 1 teaspoon of cordial to each flute of prosecco. Stir and check the flavor, adding more if needed. Serve immediately.

Mulled wine

Serves 8–10

3 clementines, halved
2 bottles red wine (Montepulciano d'Abruzzo works really well)
1 heaping cup port
2 cinnamon sticks
2 bay leaves
about ⅓ cup brown sugar
12 cloves
1 nutmeg

Gently squeeze the clementines into a pot containing the wine, port, cinnamon, bay leaves, and sugar. Stud the clementine shells with the cloves and add them. Grate in one-third of the nutmeg. Bring to just before boiling, ensuring the sugar is dissolved. Check the sweetness. Let cool a little and serve after 10–15 minutes.

Spiced cider

Serves 6

4 cups good cider
⅔ cup cider brandy
2 cinnamon sticks
about ⅓ cup superfine sugar
   (this assumes a sour cider)
6 allspice berries
1 nutmeg
1 firm apple, cored and
   cut into thick slices
12 cloves

Put the cider and brandy in a pot with the cinnamon and sugar. Bash the allspice and add. Grate in one-third of the nutmeg. Stud the apple slices with cloves and drop them in. Gently bring to just before boiling and check the sweetness. Let cool slightly and serve after 10 minutes.

Irish hot port

Serves 1

1 teaspoon brown sugar
scant 5 tablespoons port
1 unwaxed lemon slice, studded with 4 cloves

Dissolve the sugar in scant 5 tablespoons of just-boiled hot water and add the port. Lightly squeeze in the lemon slice and add the slice. Serve immediately.

Acknowledgments

This book would never have happened if people hadn't read my blog, so to all my readers, thank you!

Thanks, in particular, to my family for their unending support, especially my mother for always encouraging me to follow whatever it is that I want to do, and for buying me all of those cooking magazines when I was younger!

To Art for his unfailing faith in what I do, his honest criticism and his generous palate.

To my agent Clare for believing in what I wanted to do and helping me choose the best publisher for me, Quadrille.

To Ben, my market manager, for his incredible support and encouragement.

To Quadrille for publishing me, for being fantastically supportive, for letting me determine how this should go, particularly Anne, Mark, Clare, and Nikki.

To my editor Lucy, for her patience, support, and wisdom.

To my wonderful photographer Georgia Glynn Smith for being brilliant and encouraging, and for interpreting my style perfectly for this book.

Thank you, too, for buying this book.